To John & Sue Jan...
    God bless...
remember the Grape Nuts.)

Meredith Tales

HONEY IN THE LION

Sermons preached at Church of the Saviour, Cleveland, Ohio, and published by the Trustees of the Church in honor of ten years of ministry by Dr. Kalas, 1972 - 1982.

J. Ellsworth Kalas

The cover drawing represents a portion of the pulpit at Church of the Saviour, Cleveland, Ohio, with engravings of a number of Old Testament prophets.

Table of Contents

Preface

On the first Sunday of July, 1972, Dr. J. Ellsworth Kalas preached his first sermon as the minister of the Church of the Saviour (United Methodist), Cleveland Heights, Ohio.

During the ten years of his ministry, his sermons have been inspirational, scholarly, and a day-to-day help in our lives. Hundreds of listeners (many radio and television) have requested copies of his sermons.

The Board of Trustees of the Church of the Saviour and the Church of the Saviour Foundation in commemoration of Dr. Kalas' first ten years is making possible this publication of a group of sermons selected from the many excellent ones of those years.

We hope you will find this collection a joy and an inspiration.

G. ROBERT KLEIN

Acknowledgements

As Mr. Klein's preface indicates, this book is a celebration of ten years of ministry at the Church of the Saviour. Although many persons over the years have kindly and generously urged me to put some of my sermons into a book, I expect it would not have happened if it had not been for this concrete action by our Board of Trustees and the Church of the Saviour Foundation.

I owe particular thanks to Dr. Meredith Colket, who first suggested the idea to our Trustees; to G. Robert Klein, long-time chairman of the Trustees; and to Arthur J. Pelander, chairman of the Pastor-Parish Relations Committee.

Still more, I am indebted to Dr. Earl Anderson, Robert Morey, Linn Raney, Dr. Daniel Schubert, and John Twist, for their helpful editorial counsel and their assistance in pursuit of publishing information. Susan Sharpe and Alice Schueneman of our church staff have taken time from other responsibilities in order to type the manuscript.

My wife, Ruth, and our daughter and son, Taddy and David, have been constant in their expressions of enthusiasm for my preaching, which has been a continuing source of strength.

I am grateful, finally, to those thousands of persons in the congregations I have pastored and in scores of churches where I have held preaching missions, for the kind of attentive listening which makes a preacher rise above himself; and to our Lord Christ, who has left us with a gospel which is a joy and privilege to declare.

J. ELLSWORTH KALAS

Life's greatest blessings so often come in strange wrappings . . .

An old gospel song promises that "we'll understand it better by-and-by . . . when the morning comes, and all the saints of God are gathered home." One thing is sure, it's often difficult to recognize our blessings when first they appear. As a matter of fact, they don't always start in the guise of blessings. If anything, it appears that life deals us an unlikely mixture of raw materials, and we have to see if we can make anything of them.

That's where our faith has a chance to go to work. Working with God, we have the privilege of transforming bad news into blessing, trouble into triumph.

Honey In the Lion

Life has two kinds of riddles, those we make up and those which circumstances thrust upon us. Those which we create, as a kind of intellectual plaything, seem sometimes to serve as a diversion from the anguish of life's real and inescapable riddles.

Many centuries ago a young man made up a plaything type of riddle for his own enjoyment and in order to perplex his companions. But in the story back of his riddle, I find an insight into one of those larger riddles which we face in life itself.

You will find the story in the Old Testament book of judges. Samson, the judge of ancient Israel who is famous in folklore as the strongest man who ever lived, set out one day to court a young woman in a somewhat distant community. While traveling through the rugged countryside, he came upon a young lion. With his phenomenal strength and encouraged by the Spirit of the Lord, Samson "tore the lion asunder as one tears a kid."

Several weeks later, as he traveled that road again, he stopped to look at the carcass. Perhaps the scene delighted him, as a memory of his triumph. He found that a swarm of bees had settled in the skeleton of the lion. There were few hollow trees in that barren area, so wild bees often established their base in the skeleton of animals. The hot, dry climate would turn the carcass of an animal with its tough skin into a very satisfactory setting for a hive. By now, the carcass of Samson's lion was rich with honey. He scooped out a generous supply and went on his

11

way, eating as he went. He also gave some to his parents, although—perhaps out of respect for their more delicate sensibilities—he did not tell them from whence he had gotten the honey.

At a kind of stag party prior to his wedding, Samson followed the fashion of his day by putting a riddle to the young men who were there;

> "out of the eater came something to eat,
> Out of the strong came something sweet."[1]

The young men (and this doesn't surprise us) couldn't come up with the answer. Not, at any rate, until they got help from Samson's fiance.

I see a parable in Samson's story. He found nourishment—indeed, life—in that which had threatened to destroy him. The lion was itself an eater, but out of his carcass came something to eat. Samson found sweetness in what might have been his destruction. He found *honey in the lion.*

Blessed are those who learn that there is honey in the lion! Let there be no question about it: as we travel along the uneven paths of life, whether through its rugged wilderness or in its places of seeming civilization and sophistication, we will be confronted by lions. Some of the lions we meet are capable of destroying us. In other instances, they maul and maim us, leaving us marked for the rest of life. For those who walk a primitive road, there are the lions of violence, hunger, poverty, and desolation. For many of us, the path is superficially more peaceful. Yet there are lions in this road, too, and their ultimate terror can be altogether as great. As a matter of fact, some people in our time encounter terror in social pressure, job pressure, nerves and tension which is fully as threatening as physical violence in another culture. And for all of us, whatever road we travel, there are the lions of disappointment, disillusionment, sickness, bereavement, and death. Every human being, whatever his or her road of life, must somewhere face a lion. And again, another lion. And another.

At such times of crisis, some simply give up. They wring their hands and cry, "Why must life be like this?" Some become bitter. They clench a fist at life and become like the lion itself, as they turn to prey upon and devour others, just as they have been preyed upon. "If life is hard," they say, "I'll be hard. People have deceived me, so I'll deceive them." In a life which has its lions, they add to the ravenous destruction which walks the earth.

But others, thank God, discover the secret of Samson's parable. In the eater, they find something to eat. In the strong, they find that which is sweet. They find honey in the lion.

Believe me, there is *always* honey in the lion, but we must be willing to find it. Here is the great marvel of our universe, that out of the destruction and brutality of human beings, or out of the very tragedies of nature, we can so surely bring a harvest of good. When this happens, we marvel. After all, we would expect a law of spiritual genetics whereby sickness would bring forth more sickness, desolation a new generation of desolation, pain more pain. And left to themselves, they do. But be astonished at this, that so often out of the pain or sickness or desolation comes not more of the same, but beauty! There is honey in the lion.

Take an example from the broad stage of life, perhaps an extreme example. Surely nothing good can be said for war. Here, for sure, is a lion, a roaring, bestial thing. Yet consider the

13

honey we have found even in war. Research specialists say that World War II brought more developments in medicine during a short period of time than would have come in a whole generation of peace, especially in the development of anti-biotics. At another level, war brought a depth of camaraderie between friends which may be hard to reproduce in better times. Still more: I venture that when the intellectual history of America is written, we will discover that it was World War II and the ensuing G.I. Bill which revolutionized America's attitude toward a college education. Beginning in the late 1940's, Americans have assumed that a college education is something not for a select minority but for anyone who desires to seek it.

Or consider a monstrous factor of that same period of history, the Nazi annihilation of millions of Jews. There are few more abhorrent chapters in human history. Yet that very ugly chapter served to shock many previously thoughtless people into seeing the irrational end of race prejudice. The Nazis demonstrated that if you follow unreasoning prejudice to its limit—as they did—the only conclusion is genocide, the mass destruction of a people. Prejudice ceased then to be a casual, private matter, and became an issue of human survival.

Human history is full of the stories of individuals who have found honey in the lion. The greatest orator of ancient times (some would say, the greatest orator of human history) was Demosthenes. But Demosthenes found the honey of his oratory in a lion. He had grand thoughts and phrases, but he had a harsh voice, weak lungs, and an awkward manner. Lord, what a tragedy, to have the music of great ideas in your soul and the hunger to share them with others, but to have a devil in your speech that would make people snicker each time you open your mouth! You remember that Demosthenes recited as he climbed steep hills, that he practised speaking with pebbles in his mouth in order to develop clarity of speech, and that he spoke against the roar of the ocean to strengthen his vocal powers. I'm sure, as Randall Stewart has said, that a good college advisory system would never have allowed Demosthenes to major in speech. But Demosthenes became the classic symbol of oratory. He found honey in his lion.

So often it is this way. Blind at middle age, John Milton wrote:

> "When I consider how my light is spent
> Ere half my days in this dark world and wide . . ."

Yet in that darkness, he was most productive, giving the world *Paradise Lost* and *Paradise Regained.* John Bunyan wrote the world's greatest allegory, *Pilgrim's Progress*, not in the beauty of a scholar's study but in a dank prison cell. Beethoven envisioned a career as a concert pianist, but his growing deafness drove him into composition. Most of his great works were written as his hearing failed, and his immortal "Ninth Symphony" came when he was totally deaf.

At a very different level of life, I think of a Kansas schoolboy, Glenn Cunningham. He was burned so severely in a schoolhouse fire when he was eight years old that his doctor said he would never walk again. But the boy found the honey of courage and determination in the lion, until he was the prince of the American track. I wonder, without his lion, if Cunningham would ever have been anything more than a good, average athlete?

15

Sometimes we find our honey in another person's lion, through circumstances which cause us to make his or her lion our own. One day in his youth, Albert Schweitzer had a typical boyhood fight with a lad from a poor family. Young Schweitzer defeated the youngster, but as the poor boy ran away he cried, "If I could have soup every day as you do, I could beat you." The words made a deep impression on Schweitzer, so that he poured his life into relieving the sufferings of others. Thus the lion of a little boy's defeat helped shape a life which set peace and healing and beauty all over the world.

But we don't have to look to history or to the stories of other persons to learn the truth of what I am saying. It's altogether likely that you have met some lion and have found his store of honey. Perhaps you remember a stunning personal defeat which seemed almost to wipe out life. Yet in the defeat and its shame you gained a compassion for others which you never really knew before. Some of us remember days of painful poverty. On reflection, you wonder how your parents had the heart to go on living. You can still feel the humiliation of patched clothing and welfare food. But in the lion of that poverty you found the honey of self-reliance. And several, I'm sure, remember when sickness marched hard into your home. Until then you had taken religion pretty much for granted. But when the lion of suffering tore hard at your life and the lion of death tensed at the ready, you reached toward God as you never had before, and in your reaching came to a great faith. You found the honey of faith in the lion of despair.

You might think that I'm telling you to be strong in the face of adversity. I'm trying to say far more than that. God is the crucial factor, and our faith in Him, far beyond all our high resolves and

16

gritted teeth and earnest intentions. Sometimes, in fact, our strength may itself—ironically—get in our way. The apostle Paul was handicapped by what he called "a thorn in the flesh." Whatever it was (he never tells us), he besought God three times that it might be removed. And each time God said to him, "My grace is sufficient for you, for my power is made perfect in weakness." So Paul declared, "I will all the more gladly boast of my weaknesses, that the power of Christ may rest upon me."[2] Perhaps this is the greatest victory of all, to find honey in the lion of our weakness.

I believe there is *always* honey in the lion. We can always find something to eat in the eater, a sweetness in tragedy. The economy of God is such that from the ashes can come precious chemicals, from rot and refuse come life-giving fertilizer, from mold, a healing medicine. There is honey in the lion, sweetness in the peril of life.

But we must go after it. Samson had to confront his lion, then reach into the destroyer and take out his honey. In the same way, you and I will have to pursue the honey of life. It will not thrust itself upon us. Indeed, if we prefer to see the ghastliness of the slain lion, or if we choose to run from the struggle, or if we blind ourselves with self-pity, we can miss the sweetness which awaits us. Neither God nor life will force it upon us. The honey is in the lion for those who will say, "I know that in all things God works for my good. Therefore I look at my sickness, my disappointment, my defeat, with faith. There is honey in this lion, and some day I will have it."

I cannot help but be an optimist about life, because I believe in God. I do not ask, nor expect, that I should escape from life's issues. Sickness, death, and disappointment will sometime meet us all. But I rejoice that the lion does not have to be a destroyer. He can be a source of honey, if we will make him so.

Don't, by any means, ask for trouble. Common sense should tell us to avoid any pain which is not necessary, and human compassion tells us to do all we can to save others from suffering. But if trouble comes, grasp your lion firmly, and calling upon the Spirit of God, wrench defeat in your hands.

Then say to yourself, and in hope and thanksgiving say to God, "Some day I will pass this place, and I will look again at this carcass of destruction, this vileness that I wish had never come into my life. And though it doesn't seem possible now, I know that I will find in the frame of this destroyer a store of honey. There will be something to eat in the eater, and from the strong I will draw something sweet. By God's help, I will find honey in the lion."

What are you reading these days?

We judge the importance of books by the number of copies they sell, and most authors will agree that that's not a matter to be disregarded. But all of us also know that there are some books which attain only a limited circulation, yet have a great impact upon at least some of us.

Most of us, in making up our own list of great boods, would include a few titles which are significant for purely personal reasons. They are books which came to us at some juncture in life, or by recommendation of some special person, and thus their importance to us is beyond ordinary measure.

And then, there are some books which perhaps you've never thought of as being "great books" . . .

The Three Great Books

Some books are great because of what they tell us; others are great because of what they tell about us. The first are public books, available in bookstores and libraries; the second are usually very private.

The books which tell about us are published under only the most unusual circumstances. In most cases no one sees them except the persons who write them. Worse yet, even those who write them seldom read them. That is, they seldom read them thoughtfully enough and objectively enough to discern their message. For in the books which tell about us, the message is usually to be found between the lines and below the surface. On the surface they are likely to tell only superficial things; below the surface, they reveal the depths of human nature and of life.

Perhaps you wonder how I can say that a book is "great" when I confess that it is not a best seller; that, in fact, in most cases it will not even be published. I suggest it partly because I believe in the individual and his or her worth. I reason that if a book gives insight into a person, it possesses real greatness. And incidentally, in those few cases when some of these great books *have* been published, it's interesting to see how many have become enduring classics. I venture that this is because they come from the interior of one person with such clarity that they reach the same inner depths of many of the rest of us. Another element in the greatness of these books is that they are so readily available. Some of us have all three, most of us have two, probably everyone among us has at least one.

If we were to read these books thoughtfully, we might to a degree be relieved of the need for a psychiatrist, or at the least, we'd give him a head start on dealing with our problems. These books offer us the self-insight so many of us seem to lack. But again, it must be said that they can accomplish their potential only if we read them with openness of spirit.

The first great book (and in my judgment, the least of the three) is the *diary* or *journal*. In most cases, this book is not quite so self-revealing as the others because we're generally more self-conscious when we write it. It occurs to us that someone might well get hold of it someday, so we make guarded entries, except at times of great emotion.

Diaries aren't what they used to be. Our Puritan ancestors here in America were great diary-keepers. But for them it wasn't simply a matter of writing, "Had lunch with Jim. It was a sunshiney day and we had a marvelous time." The Puritans looked upon their journals as a spiritual exercise, a way of keeping a record of the soul's journey through earth. John Quincy Adams wasn't a Puritan, but he inherited some of the characteristics. He encouraged his son, Charles Francis Adams, to make a daily record of his life so that it might preserve his morals and be a "second conscience."

A diary can surely serve that purpose if we'll let it. Jessamyn West, the fine contemporary novelist, says that "people who keep journals have life twice." It's like talking to one's self, she points out, which while it sometimes seems peculiar, can nevertheless be very profitable. Miss West contends that no other kind of writing gives the reader so much the feel of what another person has experienced.[1]

But I'm not so interested in other people knowing what you

22

and I have experienced as I am in a self-evaluation of our own experiences. If you keep a diary, what do you learn by reading it? Your diary may not sound like Samuel Pepys', Ralph Waldo Emerson's, or Henry David Thoreau's, but it's a great book if it turns fresh light on your own soul.

Does your diary, for instance, embarrass you when you look at past pages? That may be a good sign. It may mean that you're wiser and more mature now than you were five years age. On the other hand, does it make you sad, with a wistful longing for bygone days? Were those other days far better than the present? If so, what can you do to bring a better quality into the present? Or should you, perhaps, see if you are unrealistic about the past, and ought you to be more grateful for the goodness life presently affords?

Most of all, does your diary have any spiritual content? Can God be found on its pages? Dr. Samuel Johnson wrote prayers into his journal; today, they constitute a wealth of spiritual nourishment. Are there any prayers, either structured or implied, in your diary? If someone should read your diary, would he ever guess that you are an eternal creature and that you know it?—that you have aims and purposes beyond the affairs of this earth? What would your diary reveal about the things that mean most to you, or that most absorb your attention?

The second great book is something like a diary except that it is more simple, more honest, and more revealing: your *date book* or *calendar*. Now here's a book, friend, that tells a very great deal about us. After all, it tells where a person's life is going, how it is being spent. Since life is the most precious commodity we have—in a sense, the only thing that really matters—it's important to have an accounting of the way it's being invested.

A great deal of life is spent, of course, in simply keeping alive. Take eating, for instance. Even if you eat rather rapidly, you'll spend at least 15 twenty-four hour days every year doing nothing but eating. If you live to be 70 years old, you'll spend at least three full years eating. Some of us look as if we're investing even more time in this enterprise! And sleeping: If you sleep eight hours a night, and live 70 years, you'll sleep for nearly 24 years. The only difference between you and Rip Van Winkle will be that he packed his long nap into one extended period.

But eating and sleeping are necessary to keep us alive. How about the rest of our time? You'll spend another large piece of time at work. Probably about ten years of your 70 will be given to working. Perhaps you're surprised that it isn't a bigger chunk of life, but of course we don't work all through life, as we eat and sleep. Ten years is a long sentence, at any rate, if you don't love your work or if you feel that it doesn't really matter.

But what about the rest of life? What does your date book reveal about where your life is going? On the basis of your date book, do you have any right to ask God for eternity? That is, are you using this current gift of life in such a way that you might seem to merit a longer piece on which to work?

Since I was a young man I have loved a little prayer hymn that ponders, at eventide, if one has wounded any soul today, or caused some foot to go astray, and appeals, "Dear Lord, forgive." But I remind myself that such an evaluation of my days is not penetrating enough. I ought indeed to wonder if I've done harm, and then set about to do better. But in so many instances I need also to ask another kind of question; it is not only a matter of my having spent my time doing wrong, but how much *right* have I done? As a sign on a church bulletin board puts it, "What have you done today that nobody but a Christian would do?"

In matters of your business and social life, how do you make sure you do the things which really need being done? It's very simple: you put them into your date book. So here's the question: Are you getting the truly important things into your date book? Elton Trueblood says that a person ought to go through his calendar and fill in empty places "with really important commitments, including those to meditation, to solitude, to prayer . . ."[2] Are the important things in your calendar?—such things as prayer, time to be alone with your own soul, time to write a friend, time to walk with a child? Aren't these the things that matter? But you see, many of these things will never get done unless we put them into our date books. What does it say about us if the appointment with the hairdresser is in our date book, but there's no time reserved to read the Bible, no hour set aside to commune privately with our souls?

Our date books tell so much about us. They tell how much of our lives we give to other people. They reveal what has first claim on us. They also show that while we may say that love and friendship are the most important matters in our lives, they are often lost by default, simply because we don't guarantee them a place in our lives through the date book. I don't know, of course, what will happen in the last judgment, but I have a feeling that heaven will need no more evidence in that day than a collection of our date books and calendars. From our date books both the matters which have claimed our time and the matters which are missing will reveal who was really the Lord of our lives. It's all there, in the black of what we've written in and the white of what we've left out.

There is a third great book which tells us much about ourselves: Our *checkbooks*.

This sermon really began for me when I was going through some very old checks one evening, to see if any should be saved. I intended to do so efficiently; but I soon found that sorting out cancelled checks is very much like cleaning out the attic. Before long you're lost in reminiscing over your personal history. Some checks were to persons and institutions I could no longer remember. Some were so far removed from my present life that I could easily have believed they were written by a different person.

I discovered that most of my checks had to do with keeping alive: They were written for food, clothing and utilities. I also discovered that I now spend much more to "keep alive" than I used to. "Inflation," someone says. Yes, inflation; but not simply economic inflation; more dramatically, *appetite inflation*. I realized that I now *want* more things, and *more expensive* things, than I used to.

And then I thought about John Wesley, the founder of Methodism. When he was at Oxford, his income was 30 pounds a year. He lived on 28, and gave two away. Gradually his income increased: to 60 pounds, to 90 pounds, to 120 pounds. But still he lived on 28 pounds, and gave the rest away.

Now I hasten to confess that Wesley lived in a different time. It would be very hard, in our inflationary economy, to keep living on the same amount every year. And I'm not as tough a disciplinarian as Wesley. I'm glad I can afford to eat out, glad I can sometimes go to a ballgame, a play, or a concert. I'm really very thrilled when I can see the people in my congregation enjoying what we call "the good things of life."

And yet, that check book raises some serious questions. How much am I investing in eternity? Has my concern for other people, and my love for the work of God, experienced the same inflation as the economy and my appetites? It occurs to me that when my income was $2,400. a year, ten per cent of it went to church and charity; and today, when it is substantially more, only eleven or twelve per cent is dedicated to such a purpose. Yet the amount of discretionary money—the amount available to me beyond the real basic necessities of life—is much, much more. My check book tells a story. What about yours?

Many centuries ago a wise and devout person looked at his own life against the backdrop of God's eternity. "From everlasting to everlasting thou art God," he said. "For a thousand years in thy sight are but as yesterday when it is past." And in light of that fact he prayed, "So teach us to number our days, that we may get a heart of widsom."[3] That's what we've been trying to do in this sermon. We've tried to look deep into our lives with the help of three great books: the diary, the date book, and the checkbook. And with our looking we cry, "Teach me to number my days, my appointments and my finances, so that I will live with wisdom . . . The wisdom of God's eternity."

*The town in which we live is a Divine assign-
ment . . .*

The morale of the city of Cleveland, including the suburbs
which house so many of its workers and executive leaders, was
very low in the early months of 1979. City Hall and City Council
were at a stalemate and the exodus of major firms was
threatening to become a flood. The City had declared
bankruptcy.

Our Town was one pastor's approach to that problem. The
sermon was so well received that Dr. Kalas was asked to present
the same material to the Rotary Club of Cleveland, which is one
of the half-dozen largest in the world. The talk caught fire; he
was interrupted a number of times by bursts of applause, and
when he sat down, the large audience arose in a dramatic
standing ovation.

Those selecting the sermons for this collection judged that
though this sermon is local, it belongs in the book. In mood, it
deals with problems which face many communities, and it is
particularly significant to this collection because of its impact
on greater Cleveland.

Our Town

In 1972 I was senior minister of a church in Madison, Wisconsin, a city which had several times been cited by national magazines as an ideal place in which to live. I had enjoyed ten wonderful years in that city, and could readily agree with the praise it had received. Nevertheless, when Church of the Saviour invited me, through two cooperating bishops, to become senior minister of its congregation, I felt moved to accept, though I really knew very little about Cleveland itself except that it was one of America's great, old, industrial cities.

When the newspapers in Wisconsin announced our new assignment, numbers of persons asked, "Why would you want to move to Cleveland?" That didn't surprise me; I saw it as an expression of regional pride, and the kind of response people make when they wonder why you're leaving their city for another. But I was not prepared to hear the same sort of thing in Cleveland. Indeed, I was bewildered and nonplussed when person after person here followed up introductions by asking, "What ever in the world made you move to Cleveland?"

I believe that groups, as well as individuals have a personality, a temperament, a psyche. Cleveland's is unbelievably negative. I can understand why New York is boastful; it's the biggest. And why Boston is condescending; history is on its side. But why should Cleveland have such a quality of self-loathing?

After all, Cleveland was once the most progressively

31

governed city in America. In the days of Tom Johnson, the great cities of the world studied us. Between 1880 and 1930 ours was the fastest growing city in the United States. As American industry came into its own, coal, oil, and iron were the big three—and those big three met best in Cleveland. In those days you didn't need a Growth Association to convince you that it was the best location in the nation.

What happened? What caused the downhill slide? First, let me remind you that what happened to Cleveland is not unique. Every major northern industrial and commercial city has been beset by the same problems. Rapid growth encouraged the proliferation of cheap housing which could overnight become slums. Poor zoning laws caused cities to be pockmarked with industrial and human ugliness. When good transportation made suburbia possible, those with means began to take advantage of the opportunity. Slowly and steadily, much of the strongest leadership of the city began moving into those suburbs, giving most cities a split personality: people drove into the city each day to make their money, then returned to the suburbs each evening to enjoy what they had made. And somehow most of them were blithely unaware that great suburbs could not build forever on the crumbling foundations of deteriorating cities.

Northern cities then suffered another blow. Air conditioning made southern life more palatable, and gave new potential to its labor force. As the labor situation in the north became more and more complex, the reservoir of cheaper labor in the south became attractive. And as more people moved south, the growing market made it still more attractive. Suddenly the Sun Belt was born, and northern cities had to run for their lives. But

I repeat, these problems were not unique to Cleveland.

The other day I heard a good man explain our situation by saying that Cleveland was suffering for its sins. If that were the case, I can name a dozen cities which should probably be ahead of us in the line for divine judgment. As cities go, our case is reasonably good. We are the birthplace of such honorable programs as Community Chest and Chambers of Commerce, and we still lead the nation in support of each. We were the first major city to have an open access library, and our art museum—probably the second greatest in America—is the last major museum to offer free admittance. It is popularly said that when Clevelanders awaken in the morning they first ask, "What can I do for somebody today?" When you consider our support of public improvements and community benefits, the description seems to fit. When one compares our record with that of other cities, I doubt that we are suffering because of any unique sinfulness.

But I continually ask myself what happened to Cleveland's leaders during the period of decline. Were they simply indifferent and preoccupied? Were they demoralized, so that they retreated in confusion, rather than re-grouping their forces? How is it that a city with such a body of corporate, legal, religious, cultural, educational and medical geniuses—as notable a group as one might find, in total, anywhere in America—how is it that they could let one street after another become a slum? These things did not happen overnight; they did not happen in secret. People drove by or walked in the midst of the encroaching disaster every day; why didn't they join hands to prevent it?

All right, someone replies; if you're so wise, tell us how. I wish

33

I were so wise! I am not a master economist, psychologist, or political scientist, and all these skills are needed. But let me say a few things. The first won't please many of you: we need effective regional or metro government. The 62 governing units in this county need to come under one head; for to paraphrase Benjamin Franklin, if we do not all choose to live together, it is certain that we shall all die separately. Believe me, Cleveland Heights, Parma, or Pepper Pike won't last long if Cleveland continues to deteriorate. The suburbanite says, "We don't want Cleveland's problems." Do you think you can build a fence around Cleveland, so the problems stay at the boundary of Cedar Hill? We are already one community in our problems; it's time we became one community in our commitment to solutions.

Secondly, an affirmative program of tax abatement should be written into law for at least the next decade—not only for industry and business, but for the individual home owner. Tax abatement doesn't mean that people stop paying taxes or pay less taxes; it means that those who improve property will not immediately have to pay more taxes, but that those taxes will increase slowly, by percentage, until at last the full, new value of the property is taxed. This kind of encouragement should be given to every business and homeowner, as an incentive to upgrade their properties and improve their businesses and way of life. If we do so, our tax base today will be as great as ever, and tomorrow it will be steadily larger. If we don't, tomorrow it will diminish, diminish, diminish. Thriving cities attract industry by tax abatement; *we* need it to hold what we have, to bring in more, and to encourage the average, neighborhood citizen.

I am disappointed in the Growth Association. Our community problems have called for skilled surgery; they have spread on a layer of gaudy cosmetics. Mind you, I like the lilting tune, "The Best Things in Life Are Right Here in Cleveland"; I even believe it. But the singing commercial seems to be one part narcissism, one part soap commercial, and one part whistling through the cemetery. The "New Generation" theme is equally bankrupt; it just doesn't speak to our needs. It may be well-meaning, but it is superficial and inept.

As for the media, I have "three things against them, yea, four," as the prophet Amos would say. I know that newspapers and television reporters tell us that they don't make the news, they only report it; but this is a bit too pious and irresponsible. Media control the news in at least two ways: they decide what news to report, since there isn't space or time for all of it, and they decide the style and degree of importance with which it shall be reported. The editorial page professes responsible loyalty to Cleveland; the news headlines destroy us.

Let me give a few examples. Several weeks ago a new baseball player, Toby Harrah, came to Cleveland by trade. The young man expressed pleasure in coming here. The *Plain Dealer* headline said, "Harrah is a rarity; he likes Cleveland." At about the same time John Gelbach, chairman of the Growth Association, gave a major speech in which he analyzed our city. He reported that employment is at an all-time high, that downtown construction has surpassed that of Dallas, Denver, Minneapolis, and Baltimore in a recent five-year period, and that our average household income is higher than the U.S. as a whole and above such cities as Boston, Philadelphia, Atlanta, Los Angeles, and New York. He analyzed our problems and suggested solutions. He promised a new approach from the

Growth Association. The *Cleveland Press* headlined the story, "Gelbach zeroes in on the city's woes." A firm moves out of Cleveland, and the *Plain Dealer* reports it on the front page; a firm moves in, or a major employer hires a thousand more employees, and they feature the story in the business section. The problem, you see, is that the public climate is set by headlines, not in-depth reporting, and the most prominent headlines make the greatest impact. Our good news should be front page news. As for many of the radio and television weather personalities, I just don't have the patience to tell you what I think of their limited sense of humor. What we need from the media is not a jingle campaign, and not soft soap, but a vigorously *positive* approach to the facts.

Our community leadership is in many ways unsurpassed. I'm not sure, however, that they are putting their energy in the places of greatest need. Some of my most heartfelt pride in Cleveland is in its unexcelled cultural benefits: museums, libraries, parks, orchestra, universities, drama centers—an awesome list. But sometimes as I glory in these benefits, I think of Baalbek, Luxor, and Petra—architectural wonders of the ancient world which now lie in deserted wilderness. Is it possible that public benefactors in their day built these at the neglect of common human need around them? I would not remotely suggest that we should neglect our cultural centers; but I submit that some of the leadership and energy which have gone into these centers could so profitably be invested in redeeming the hundreds of blocks of ramshackle houses and ghetto surrounding them. Otherwise we may someday be forced to drive through a wilderness to get to these places. Indeed, such is already the case. The same skills which have gotten us the museum, the Orchestra, and the Play House can heal our slums. And if expert, experienced help is needed, we can call on Sister Henrietta!

Sermons sometimes leave the average listener frustrated, in not knowing what he or she personally can do, except feel frustrated! Herewith, some practical, simple suggestions: Support those organizations which better our city; you can't belong to everything, but buy memberships where you can. Accentuate the positive: if you're sending a gift to someone out of town, send them a recording of the Cleveland Orchestra or a book or print from the Cleveland Museum of Art. Buy Cleveland; sell Cleveland. Every time you have a chance, say a good word for Cleveland; and every time some newspaper, comedian, or television commentator mishandles us, express your displeasure, firmly and intelligently. I'm not a bumper sticker type, but if someone would print a sticker that said, "I Choose Cleveland"—a positive, succinct statement of the way many of us feel about this city—I'd put it on my automobile. Indeed, if I weren't so reserved, I'd even paste it on my traveling bag, to announce my feelings wherever I go.

For thirty years I have been captivated by Katharine Lee Bates' hymn poem, "O Beautiful for Spacious Skies," especially its fourth verse:

> O beautiful for patriot dream
> That sees beyond the years
> Thine alabaster cities gleam,
> Undimmed by human tears.

That dream has never come true. Our cities are far from alabaster, and they are tragically flawed by human tears. But I dream that we could make it happen in Cleveland. With our

37

all-American combination of 18th century Connecticut Yankees, 19th century European ethnics, and 20th century blacks; with a city which is big enough to have everything yet small enough to make those benefits available to all its citizenry; with our full complement of big league sports, education, music, drama, and medicine; with some of the world's most beautiful neighborhoods and churches; with all of this, we have some of the most generous and dedicated citizenry to be found anywhere. We might, just yet, build an alabaster city, a place good for *all* the people who live in it.

Above all else, we have a spiritual problem. We need a revival of faith which will make our ethnics and blacks realize that their enemies are not each other, but the politicans who exploit their differences. We need a revival of faith which will make us care about the poor and disadvantaged of our city until we find a way to lead them to a better life. We need faith to see that our problems are not as big as our resources and our potential.

Twenty-five centuries ago a remarkable man named Nehemiah returned to his beloved city of Jerusalem and found it in ruins. One night he took a few companions and walked through the city; saw its hopeless rubble, its gates destroyed by fire. Then he called together the leaders of the community and said, "You see the trouble we are in, how Jerusalem lies in ruins with its gates burned. Come, let us build the wall of Jerusalem, that we may no longer suffer disgrace." Then he told how the hand of God was upon him. When he had finished, the people said, "*Let us rise up and build.*" And they succeeded, because, as Nehemiah said, "The people had a mind to work."

That's what I want to say to you just now: *Let us rise up and build.* If we will, God will be with us.

38

Why should there be so much pain in the world?

Perhaps no question is so troublesome as the question of pain and suffering; or as theologians and philosophers put it, the problem of evil. Why is there so much pain? Why, on this earth, do the innocent suffer along with the guilty? And why do good people seem sometimes to get more than their share of "bad breaks"?

Hundreds of books have been written to deal with this theme, so no single sermon can answer all the questions. But here is the way the problem was dealt with one Sunday morning.

Can God Be Good When Life Is Bad?

Several years ago I received a letter from a woman who had been a member of a church where I was the pastor. I'd like for you to read the letter, not because it is extraordinary or unique, but because it raises a question so many others have asked. Almost anyone might have written this letter, if not for themselves, then for someone else.

> Dear Rev. Kalas:
> I am still at a loss . . . who can answer my question.
> Why???—After all the years that I was so unhappy and then I met Jim and had all the happiness any one would want did "God" take him from me. If during my life I hadn't met "God" I would feel there was not a God. but some times I doubt it. I never knew life could be so lonely.
> Can you give me the answer.—

This is the question which, at one time or another, almost everyone asks: *Why?* When my correspondent wrote the word she followed it with three question marks, as if she were addressing the question to each member of the Trinity: Why??? Why does life sometimes take such perplexing, agonizing, irrational turns? Why, if God is good? When a baby is born into the world fearfully handicapped, when a little child is killed by a freakish accident, when a good, kind human being is immobilized by devastating illness at the height of life, where does God fit into the picture? Can God be good when life is bad?

41

Before I go to the heart of the question, let me eliminate from our consideration those misfortunes for which we are ourselves responsible. The person who has indigestion from overeating cannot rightly blame God for his troubles; neither should we blame God in numbers of other cases. When a man becomes intoxicated and drives his car into a tree, he needn't ask, "Why did God do this to me?" When a woman neglects her husband and family and her home breaks up, she shouldn't ask, "Why did God allow such a thing?" When a boy doesn't crack a book all semester, then fails the final exam, he shouldn't ask, "How can God treat me this way?" Many of our illnesses are the result of our own excesses or neglects; much of the anguish in our family and social relationships springs from our own errors of judgment; many of our financial distresses are a result of our own carelessness. We have no business blaming God for such problems.

The same thing can be said of some of our larger problems. "Why does God allow war?" people sometimes ask—as if God manufactured munitions and flew bomber planes, as if angels were scattering napalm. God doesn't start wars; human beings wage wars. So, too, with much poverty. Agricultural specialists say our world is capable of feeding all of the world's present population. It is our human failure, in politics and economics, that allows thousands to starve and millions to be ill–fed.

In fact, we should thank God, not blame Him, that suffering follows our sins and stupidity. If bad did not result from our human sinfulness, it would be hard to believe in the goodness of God. I would not want God to wink at injustice and selfishness. The universe would be a nightmare if there were not written into it some sense of rightness. When we see that selfishness and sin come to judgment, even in this life, it is easier to believe in ultimate justice.

But what about those tragedies which are not a direct result of our own sins or our wrong decisions? Granted that war is a product of man's own iniquity—but why must *your* loved one be lost in battle or permanently injured? And what shall we say of the natural disasters, which seem to operate without any rational pattern? Who can explain the tornado which skips capriciously through an area, leaping over one home, so that its inhabitants thank God for safety, then picking up the next and destroying it? Or what shall we say to the father whose lawnmower throws a piece of metal from the grass into the forehead of his pre-school child, causing almost instant death? What about such instances?

There are several answers I refuse to give. I will not say, nor does any one have the right to say, that the cause of human tragedy can always be traced to that person's sins. I know of nothing more pathetic than parents, already heartbroken over a tragic birth, who then add to their misery a burden of guilt by concluding that the tragedy is a punishment of God. When some of the people of Jesus' day pointed to a person handicapped from birth and asked, "Who sinned, this man or his parents, that he was born blind?", Jesus replied, "Neither one." True, much of our heartache we bring upon ourselves. But it is a violation of the Scriptures and it is a defamation of the character of God to explain human tragedy by saying that God is punishing a particular sinner.

Neither do I believe that everything which happens in our world is the will of God. After an accident or a death, I sometimes hear people say, "It must have been the will of God

43

or it wouldn't have happened." I'm sure some find consolation in such an attitude. But from what I know of the Bible, and from what I understand of the nature of God, I cannot believe that everything which happens is God's will. Indeed, it seems very clear that much of what goes on in our world is the very *opposite* of what God wants. Our Lord wept over the city of Jerusalem because that city had rejected the will of God. When Jesus prayed in the Garden of Gethsemane the night before His crucifixion, it was that the will of God might be done; Jesus recognized that the contrary was possible. When Jesus gave us a prayer, it included the phrase, "Thy will be done, on earth as it is in heaven." There should be no need to pray for the will of God if the will of God were going to be done regardless.

The truth is, the will of God will *not* be done in our world unless some of us pray and work to bring it to pass. When I see great human tragedy, I must not abdicate by saying, "It must be the will of God." Rather, I should make a new vow to God that I will do my best to help bring His will to pass. Indeed, we might well say that one of our primary assignments as Christians is to help bring God's will to our world.

But what can we say, then, about the problem of human tragedy? Why does a plague skip one family and strike the next? What determines the lightning's target? Who guides the flying shrapnel, that it misses one man and maims another?

My answer may not at first satisfy you, but I dare to state it. There is an impersonal element in much of what happens in our world, both good and bad. Jesus said that God makes His sun rise on the evil and on the good, and sends His rain on the just and on the unjust. One might go on to say that the cyclone and the pleasant breeze, the drought and the abundance, come

44

upon both the just and the unjust, and that sickness and death eventually enter every home. I do not believe that God directs all these happenings—"Here, storm, hit Joe's house"—but rather that they are a natural development within the framework of our universe and its laws. This means that those tragedies which are not a product of our own folly are impersonal. The ice on the highway was not there to skid a particular car, the bullet at Kent State did not bear a certain student's name, the flu epidemic is not aimed at a select 1,317 persons.

Now in a sense, the story stops right there for the person who lives outside of faith. But there's another chapter, a crucially important chapter, for the person who walks by faith. For right in the midst of an impersonal universe, the man and woman of faith meet a *personal* God.

Sometimes He shows Himself as a personal God by delivering in the way we have desired. Our universe operates within laws, in answer to prayer. I don't think God interferes with the ordered running of His universe, however, until we call upon Him to do so. He must determine, in His infinite wisdom, when to reply affirmatively to our prayers and when to alter them. Surely our universe would soon be a chaos if God affirmed our prayers promiscuously. But He often intervenes in such a way that we can say—and even detached observers must say—that what has happened is a kind of miracle: the miracle of a personal God becoming involved in the affairs of earth.

Furthermore, in the midst of tragedy the person of faith meets a personal God who gives grace to all who seek it—the grace to endure. Dr. William A. Spurrier says that in a sense the Old Testament book of Job is a conversation in which God says to Job, "Would you rather have the intellectual answer to your

45

problem, or the power to endure suffering?"—and Job chooses the latter. Most people who have experienced great suffering have made the same choice. In fact, I have so often been impressed that the people who have suffered most intensely have become, not the greatest atheists, but the greatest saints. In the midst of circumstances which are beyond explanation, they have found the One who is the Answer. While battered by impersonal tragedy, they have been restored by the personal God.

But there's still more to be said. In the midst of disappointment and tragedy, the believer finds a personal God *who brings good out of evil*. I believe this should happen without fail, for those who approach life with faith.

I said earlier that not everything which happens in our universe is a fulfillment of the will of God. Now let me say that God so works in the life of the believer that He fits even the elements of disaster into a mosaic of beauty. I believe this because it has happened repeatedly in my own life. I believe it because I have seen it so many times in the lives of others. I believe it because it is taught in the Scriptures. The Epistle to the Romans states it perfectly. "We know that in everything God works for good with those who love Him."[1] In *everything* God is working for good in your life, if you will cooperate with Him. He does not send the disaster, the disappointment, the failure, the heartbreak; but He brings an element into your life which transforms even such pain into blessing. I cannot promise that you will never have sickness or disappointment, but I *can* promise that God will bring good out of such experiences. I cannot promise that you will never shed tears of sorrow, but I *can* promise that your weeping can be turned into

46

a song of praise and thanksgiving.

The Apostle Paul came to the place where he could sing about his sorrows. "We rejoice in our sufferings," he said, "knowing that suffering produces endurance, and endurance produces character, and character produces hope, and hope does not disappoint us."[2] He had learned that for the Christian, suffering is not a dead end street. It is a remarkable highway, which one day turns a corner and becomes a street named Endurance; and another day, Endurance becomes Character; and yet again, Character becomes *Hope*. And in our Hope we are never disappointed. What a way to take hold of life!

Jesus often said that He must continue the work which the Father had given Him to do. Each of us ought to embrace the same resolve. There is work to be done in our world. The universe isn't finished. We should work with God to make it better. Much of the suffering in our world is caused by human beings: war and poverty, crime and pollution, hurt feelings and broken hearts. We should do what we can to eliminate such suffering. And the rest of the suffering—the irrational, impersonal things that happen—can be made much less painful if you and I will seek to comfort those who mourn and to bind up the brokenhearted. There is still work to be done in our world, work which will help bring the will of God to pass.

Can God be good when life is bad? Yes, yes indeed. In fact, we may never fully know how good God is, how ready to answer prayer, how loving and how able to help us, until we come to one of life's hard places. When life is at its worst, faith is at its best. In the dark night of the soul, the light of God breaks forth into the most glorious morning.

47

If God cares so much, dare I be uncaring?

Dr. Kalas says that "everything is grist for the preacher's mill," and several sermons in this book suggest that he lives by that rule. A popular song, a chance conversation, a line of poetry, a paragraph in the sports section may set the mind and spirit to going, with the end product appearing far down the road come Sunday morning.

In this instance, it was a stage play. The preacher had gone a bit unwillingly. He had a prior notion that the subject matter probably wouldn't interest him. But they had a series ticket, so rather than waste the money, he decided to gamble further with the investment of a Saturday afternoon. What follows is part of the result of that day.

To Whom It May Concern

Several years ago I came upon a new name for God. I intend no irreverence in what I say, only thanksgiving. The Old Testament reports numbers of instances when believers suggested new names for God as a result of their faith-experiences with Him. So, for instance, when the slave woman Hagar was sustained by God when she was lost and apparently forsaken, she called the Lord, "El-roi:" "Thou God seest me."[1] And when Gideon found peace in the midst of his very human terror, he called God "Yahweh-shalom:" "The Lord is peace."[2]

The new name that impressed itself on me came from what some would consider an unlikely place, Paul Osborne's stage play, *The World of Suzie Wong*. This is the story, as you may remember, of a prostitute on the Hong Kong waterfront. Suzie lived out her poor life in a brutal and hazardous world, but she had one consuming joy, her baby boy. One day, however, in the season when Hong Kong's rains are an endless flood, Suzie's house was washed away, and with it her little boy. When at last the baby was found, he was dead, his tiny body mangled by the storm.

In the manner of her people, Suzie prepared ceremonial papers for the burial of her child. But something was missing. She had wanted so earnestly for her little boy to grow up to be more than a coolie. Now she felt it was important to let someone in the next world know her dreams and her plans. So Suzie asked her American artist friend, Robert Lomax, to write a letter

51

to accompany the body of her boy to the next world. "Address it," Suzie said, "to that very important person, 'To Whom It May Concern.'"

Suzie, the yum-yum girl, the waterfront tart, knew little theology and probably nothing of Christianity, but she had cut through to the heart of the matter. *To Whom It May Concern.* She had found a right name for God. He is the One who is always concerned. He is the One who cares.

I'm sure the Apostle Paul would have understood Suzie. When he came to the city of Athens, there were so many images and altars that it was said to be easier to meet a god on the city streets than a man. Not only were there altars to hundreds of gods to which the Greeks had given names, there were also many altars which bore the inscription, "To an Unknown God."

It looked as if the people of Athens were trying thus to cover all theological bases, to be sure they didn't offend any possible deity by oversight. Paul might have mocked such childish superstition, or he might have rebuked the almost incredible polytheism which he found. Instead, he saw the pathos of the matter. Perhaps he knew that the Athenians had erected these altars to "the unknown god" some six hundred years before, when they were trying to stop a pestilence which had settled upon the city. At any rate, he seemed to sense that for these people the universe was an unfriendly mystery, and whatever gods there might be were such a confusion and threat that the people would reach out half-hopefully to even "an unknown god."

So Paul stood on Mars Hill, amid the majesty of the Parthenon, and cried out, "Men of Athens, I perceive that in every way you are very religious. For as I passed along, and observed the objects of your worship, I found also an altar with this inscription, 'To an unknown god.' What therefore you worship as unknown, this I proclaim to you."[3] He did not mock their bewildered groping; instead, he acknowledged that it was a basic hunger for the eternal God. Then he continued, "God is not far from each one of us, for 'In him we live and move and have our being.'"[4] Paul was telling them that in our universe there is One who cares, who has a heart for us. And He is not far off, detached and unapproachable, for "in Him we live and move and have our being."

What Paul said to the Athenians, I think he would say to Suzie Wong. He would not laugh at her simple means of expression. "To Whom It May Concern": Suzie knew only that this was a phrase she had heard used by knowing people, and it seemed logical to her that such a grand personage, whoever it might be, would be the best one to approach in her time of ultimate need. I think Paul would have said, "This one whom you address so abstractly—He is not far away, He is no impersonal legal phrase, He is the One who planted breath and longing in your bosom. He is so near that you can call Him *Father*. And yes, He *is* concerned, because He cares about you."

What Paul said to the Athenians, and what he would say to Suzie Wong, just as surely he would say to us. Our world, after all, is not really so different from the world of Suzie Wong. Our streets are different, of course, from the hurly-burly of Suzie Wong's waterfront, and our homes are far removed from her dismal quarters. But when the floods of life take from us someone we love dearly, or when the troubles of life beat us into near hopelessness, we are no different from Suzie Wong. The

53

heart breaks with the same anguish in Hong Kong or in Cleveland. And when it breaks, and wherever, we need to know that Someone is concerned, that some arms in the universe will embrace us.

Many will tell you that this is a hard world in which nobody cares. They will insist that life is a battle for survival and that the person who expects somebody in either heaven or earth to be concerned is sure to be bitterly disappointed, because no one is likely to care.

But the Bible and the Christian faith say differently. They tell us that there is One Who is concerned, and He has the power to make His concern effective. Nearly every chapter of the Old Testament shows God intervening in the affairs of both nations and individuals, intervening because He cares. The Old Testament doesn't spend a great deal of time telling us what God is like; it simply shows Him at work.

God's involvement in our human need is brought to a dramatic climax in the coming of Jesus Christ. The basic theme of the New Testament is that God is so deeply concerned that He sends His Son to walk among us, where He can know at first hand our pain and need. More than that, eventually He dies on the cross to break the power of our tragedy and to save us.

Let Suzie Wong come to the cross, then, with her letter addressed "To Whom It May Concern." Let the philosophers of Athens come, too, who think the gods are far off, unknown and uncaring. Bring these also to the Cross: the tough, sophisticated ones who say life is a battle for survival and that no one in earth or heaven is concerned. And bring the forlorn and forsaken, the bitter and the disillusioned, the lonely and the distraught. Show them, out there on the bleakness of Golgotha,

54

a Cross; and say, "Do you wonder if anyone cares? Believe me, *God* cares, and this is *how much* He cares. This is His world and He loves it; and you are His, and He loves you, even when you have wandered from Him."

But when you believe that Someone in our universe is concerned—that *God* is concerned—you are brought under obligation. If God is concerned, you and I must be concerned. Some of those who say that nobody in our world cares use this attitude as a defense against involving themselves in other people's pain. As long as we believe we live in an unconcerned universe, we may think we can excuse ourselves from feeling any concern.

But if God cares, then I must care. If God is hurt by the hurt of the world, then I must be hurt by it. If He is concerned, I must be concerned. I don't think it's possible for us really to know that God is concerned about earth's sorrows and yet go unconcerned ourselves. When I see church members who are untouched by the world's need, I fear that their Christian faith has never fully gotten through to them.

Does anybody care? One hundred twenty-five years ago nursing was not considered a respectable occupation for a woman of gentle character. But in 1854 Florence Nightingale was struck by the New Testament teaching that the kingdom of God is within us, and she accepted the call to work among British troops in the Crimean War. A daughter of wealthy parents, raised in luxury and refinement, she had previously entered nursing in spite of all the objections of the people of her class. Many told her that British soldiers were no better than animals and that she should never waste herself in caring for them. Yet with 38 nurses she brought mercy and healing to the battlefield. When her hospital was soundly organized, she began classes in which convalescent soldiers could be taught to read and write. To Whom It May Concern: it concerned God, so it concerned Florence Nightingale.

Does anybody care? Just over a century ago as urban America began to crowd and grow, young men from the country moved into the cities in hopeful droves. But they were naive and provincial, and were easy prey for unscrupulous employers and for confidence men and for women of the street. It became almost a rule of thumb that a boy coming to the city from a farm would soon lose both his money and his character.

Some people shook their heads in distress. But some others—men like John Wanamaker, Amos Lawrence, and George Stuart—were concerned. Out of their concern, the American branch of the Young Men's Christian Association rose up to save and nurture the young man in the city. Wanamaker, Lawrence, Stuart, men whose hearts had been stirred in the religious revival of 1857-58, felt they must be concerned because God was concerned.

In nineteenth century England, the woman of the streets was one of civilization's most pathetic creatures. Did anyone care about her? Some crossed the street to avoid her defilement, and others exploited her offer. But one remarkable person cared—the great Christian statesman, William Gladstone. Even while he was prime minister of the British Empire, Gladstone would go out into the streets and reason with the women, sometimes taking them to his own home where his wife, a person of equal heart and conscience, would help bring them to salvation and responsibility. God was concerned, so William Gladstone had to be concerned.

Does anybody care that there are filth and disease in Hong Kong, starvation in India, and famine in North Africa? Does anybody care that the man in your club is an alcoholic, and that the woman just down the block is a lonely, irritable neurotic? Does anybody care that there are young people and adults in the neighborhood who are without a church and a saving knowledge of God?

Now hear me: *God* cares—and therefore you and I must care. It concerns *Him*, so it must concern *us*.

Hear, then, this name for God: "To Whom It May Concern." It is a name which brings comfort and hope when we feel alone, when we are sick, disheartened, afraid. At those times when we wonder if anyone cares about us, the answer is clear: God cares. We have a concerned God.

At the same time, this name reminds us that we are to extend God's caring to others. Those of us who have glimpsed the mercy and lovingkindness of God must pass it on. We cannot follow the One who is concerned without ourselves taking on the burden of concern. We must become channels for the concern of God.

Like Suzie Wong, I would write a letter—to that "very important person, 'To Whom It May Concern.'" What a wonderful Lord He is! All that we are, all that we feel and dream and hope—all are a concern to Him.

How can anything so small be so troublesome?

". . . the tongue is a little member, and boasteth great things. Behold, how great a matter a little fire kindleth! And the tongue is a fire, a world of iniquity; . . For every kind of beasts, and of birds, and of serpents and of things in the sea, is tamed, and hath been tamed of mankind: But the tongue can no man tame . . . Therewith bless we God . . . and therewith curse we men, which are made after the similitude of God . . . These things ought not so to be."

(James 2:3, selected verses; King James Version)

59

The Tongue And I

My tongue and I have been living together for more than fifty years. We've had a lively relationship, but at times it has been a trying one.

The first few years weren't difficult, because no one held me responsible for what I did with my tongue. In fact, it seemed I could do no wrong. Everything I said seemed to delight my parents. They were astonished at each new word, almost as if I were a fount of wisdom. Often they could hardly wait to report to friends and relatives about the triumphs of my tongue.

One day, however, there was a sharp change. It happened when I repeated, under other circumstances, something which my parents had considered "cute." Buoyed by the success of my tongue, I ventured the same performance later that day in front of visitors. This time, to my surprise, it brought a reprimand. That was the day I began to learn that in all my lifetime I would face no greater task than the proper use and control of my tongue.

Gradually, I learned that with the tongue I not only can hurt the person with whom I speak, I can even hurt someone who isn't present. This means that the tongue has power beyond any physical weapon. With the tongue I can hurt great causes. With it I can injure goodness and love and faith and hope. Indeed, in a sense I can even hurt God, or at least causes and persons which are cherished by God.

Don't think I exaggerate the power of the tongue. Wiser persons have made the same point. The author of Proverbs wrote, "Death and life are in the power of the tongue."[1] The Book of Proverbs contains warnings against the dangers and sins of the tongue in almost every chapter. The wise man knew by painful experience, I venture! C. S. Lewis said that the book of Psalms mentions hardly any evil more often than misuse of the tongue. The Apostle James describes the tongue as "a fire, a world of iniquity"; and he notes that while humanity has been able to bring every kind of beast, bird, serpent and creature of the sea under control, he has not yet been able to tame the tongue, "an unruly evil, full of deadly poison." A contemporary writer might add that we have been able to bring space, electricity, atom and hydrogen under control—but not yet the tongue.

Let's consider some of the problems of the tongue. We might begin at an obvious level, the sin of saying things which are not true. It shouldn't be necessary to spend much time on this matter, for honesty is the most basic of qualities. If a person's word can't be depended upon, what can? But I am shocked, again and again, at how casually we sometimes use the truth, giving just a twist here and an exaggeration there, until we have changed the whole effect. Surely there is such a thing as truth of intention as well as truth in actual expression. When we tell something in such a way that it is likely to be misinterpreted, we cannot really claim to be thoroughly honest, for we have the intention of a lie even though we may avoid its actual form.

We can be parties to dishonesty by repeating information for which we have no adequate certainty. Do you ever find yourself saying something like, "I don't really know if this is true, but here's what Joe told me." In many instances, such a report may not be harmful, but often it is. And of course, much of the time we don't even bother to preface our statements with a disclaimer about their veracity; we simply repeat what we've heard, giving it all the authority of truth.

But a statement doesn't have to be untrue in order to be unworthy. Some things which are true still ought not to be said, because they are unkind and destructive. Some people justify this kind of talk by saying, "I believe in being frank." That treasured frankness may cloak an inner meanness. The New Testament tells us that there are some things of which it is a shame even to speak. Things may be true, yet also be corrupting and degrading, harmful to the person who speaks, to the hearer, and to the one about whom we have spoken.

In the changing styles of the times, we are currently caught up in a fad of frankness. In the opinion of many, including some in literary and entertainment circles, there is virtue in the public use of profanity and scatological language. They suggest that if such language expresses your emotions, it would be dishonest not to use it publicly. The fallacy in their reasoning is clear. It disregards the feelings and rights of others. People who are considerate of others ask themselves what their conduct will do to those who are with them. It is one of the most serious condemnations of our times that we have become indifferent to other people in matters of taste in language. We have made frankness a greater virtue than thoughtfulness.

Another problem of the tongue is that we talk too much. Dr. Konrad Adenauer once said, "Sometimes I doubt whether there is divine justice. All parts of the human body get tired eventually—except the tongue. And I feel this is unjust." Isn't it strange?—no matter how long we talk, our tongues never grow

63

weary. The voice may give out after a few hours, and the mind may have given up before that (though without our knowing it), but the tongue goes merrily on.

The wise writer of Proverbs warns us, "In the multitude of words, there wanteth not sin."[2] That is, if you keep talking long enough, you're sure eventually to say the wrong thing. A colloquial translation of the Bible puts it this way: "Don't talk so much. You keep putting your foot in your mouth. Be sensible and turn off the flow!"[3] How many times in my life I wish I had "turned off the flow" sooner than I did! In my youth I knew a godly man who said, "I sometime pray, as I leave a conversation, that people will forget what I have said." Believe me, I have often offered the same prayer.

Even good people, if they talk long enough, will say the wrong thing. Partly, this is because as we continue talking we become more casual and unrestrained—which, of course, is a good thing in many ways, but carried too far, can become bad. It's partly because human nature eggs us on to top the other person, and for that matter, to top ourselves. Has the other person said a shocking thing? Then I'll be more shocking. Did my last bit of humor evoke laughter? Then this time I'll have to get more laughter even if I abandon good taste in order to do so.

The average American speaks 26,000 words a day. There's no doubt some of us go over our quota. The finest thing some people could do would be to cut verbal production by perhaps fifty per cent. If they did, they'd cut their troubles by seventy five per cent! All of us ought to ask ourselves how many of our 26,000 words are trivial, how many are unnecessary, how many are questionable, and how many are downright harmful. And by painful contrast, we should ask how many are spiritually productive and how many bring blessing and gladness to others.

When one thinks of all the harm which can be done by talking too much, we may conclude that the best thing is to give up speech altogether. Thus some wise man said, "A man may regret his speech; never his silence." But this is not true. Sometimes silence can be a sin of the tongue altogether as evil as the ill-spoken word. That is, there is the danger that we will be silent when we ought to speak. When a person's reputation is being maligned, when a lie is told, when a great truth is discredited, it is a wicked thing to remain silent. For many of us, evil silence is even more of a danger than careless speech.

This was the sin of Germany in the 1930's, that good people remained silent when the Jews were persecuted. This is the sin of genteel people, who would rather allow a reputation to be tarnished than to disturb a dinner conversation. This is the sin of timid people, who act as if they have no convictions when they fear they will be laughed at, or thought corny or naive. By our silence we can become party to a crime.

Thus, if we are sometimes in danger of talking too much, we are in as much danger, under other circumstances, of talking too little. The tongue is a power to be used well, not to be overused, misused, or abandoned. To abandon God's gift of speech is as evil as to abuse it.

Buckminster Fuller, the twentieth century Renaissance man, frequently instructs an audience, "Stick your tongue way out before a mirror. It is a strange device. If you were tongueless and someone came offering to sell you a tongue, would you buy such a thing?" In some of life's darker moments, we think we'd gladly sell it to even the lowest bidder. But on reflection we know that the tongue, however strange its appearance, is almost priceless. The power of speech identifies us as human beings. The tongue is the major transmitter of thought. Personality is the quality of the divine, and speech is the single most significant mark of personality.

Jesus put the power and importance of the tongue in eternal terms. He warned, "On the day of judgment men will render account for every careless word they utter; for by your words you will be justified, and by your words you will be condemned."[4]

The tongue is related to so many of our weaknesses. It is a faithful slave to our pride. It can verbalize our lust. It is the noisy proclaimer of our stupidities. Isn't it strange that the tongue can charge ahead at such a breakneck speed when the brain itself is stumbling along? Surely we need help if we are to master this unruly instrument!

So what shall we do with such a powerful instrument as this, something which can bless and curse humanity, and which will be a basis for our judgment before God? Surely we have to approach it with humility, admitting that we have sometimes misused its power and that we continue to be in danger of doing so. The Apostle said that if a person does not sin with his tongue, he is perfect. I expect not many of us would claim that kind of perfection; and if we did, no doubt someone who knows us would be quick to set the record straight.

Many centuries ago a brilliant young man named Isaiah came one day to the holy temple. There he received a vision of God. As he comprehended the majesty and holiness of God, one thing struck him, above all else: the evil of his speech. Of all the matters which might have distressed him, this one dominated:

"Woe is me! For I am lost; for I am a man of unclean lips, and I dwell in the midst of a people of unclean lips."[5]

At that moment a divine messenger came to Isaiah, carrying a burning coal from the altar of the temple. With it the angel touched Isaiah's mouth, saying, "Behold, this has touched your lips; your guilt is taken away, and your sin forgiven."

Does fire seem too harsh a cure? Not when we remember that the tongue itself, as James said, is a flame of destruction. In my best moments, I cherish such a cleansing, fearful though it may be. I pray it is your desire as well.

Our tongues are capable of almost unlimited blessings if only we can see them set free. With these tongues we can speak words of hope, with them we can console, with them we can plead for great causes. The tongue can be a channel of love, of inspiration, of strength.

But if it is to be so, it must be redeemed. Grant, O God, such a cleansing, that we may be instruments of Thy love and peace.

Our search for identity . . .

Who am I? What is my purpose in life? Other generations have asked these questions, but perhaps primarily among the philosophers. In our time, the question has become a commonplace. We may some day come to the place where an infant's first words will be a complete sentence: "I'd like to find out who I am."

The secular world has a variety of answers. Some are helpful and many are sincere enough; but ultimately, we need an answer from *beyond* this world, in order to realize the full potential *of* this world. Most of us are likely to sell ourselves short. We can never fully realize all we were meant to be, except as we meet Jesus, the Christ. That's why salvation deals not only with the world to come, but also with the world in which we live right here, right now.

I've Gotta Be Me?

I'm always interested in what people are singing, or the music to which they listen. Someone said over a century ago that they didn't care who wrote the laws of a land if they could write its music. Which is to say that music is a powerful influence in nearly all our lives. It can capture our minds with its lyrics, our emotions with its melody, and our wills with its beat. I like to know what people are singing because music reveals so much about what they are—what they think, what they feel, what they dream.

I confess that I'm not much of an authority on the hit parade. Not since the days of Snooky Lanson, Giselle McKenzie, and Dorothy Collins! But I pay a good deal of attention to contemporary favorites on the car radio as I go about my pastoral work. Some of the music apparently has great appeal to some people (another generation, I expect!) though I can't always understand why. And just as surely, some music which delights me is of no interest to others.

But now and then a song comes on the scene which seems to appeal to almost everyone. Not only does it find a place in the shifting tides of the hit parade, it will manage to come back again and again over the years. A disc jockey friend tells me that such songs become known as "standards"—that is, songs which are part of the recurring material of records and performers, so that the disc jockey always keeps them in reach, regardless of passing hits and fads.

That's the case with a song from a Broadway musical of some years ago:

"Whether I'm right, or whether I'm wrong
Whether I find a place in this world, or never belong,
I've gotta be me! I've gotta be me!
What else can I be but what I am?"[1]

The writer/performer goes on to appeal for a life which is more than mere surviving, the holding to a dream that keeps one alive. He vows that he "won't settle down, or settle for less." He's ready even to "go it alone," because he's sure that "I can't be right for somebody else if I'm not right for me." I've gotta be me!

I'm sure the continuing popularity of this song is a result not only of attractive music and its presentation by outstanding performers, but especially because it voices the unspoken cry of so many persons. It may well be the most pervasive personal cry of our times. So many have a feeling that they can't be what they want to be. Young people blame it on their parents or on the schools. Adults blame it on their jobs or their families, or that indefinable something called "the system." "People won't let me be myself," someone complains. "They're always trying to press me into a mold." And so they agree with the theme of the song: "I've gotta be me! I can't be right for somebody else if I'm not right for me."

And I feel they're right. You _do_ have to be you. For me, this is not only a sociological or a psychological theory, it is a religious conviction. I believe God made you and me with utter distinctiveness. There's no one else like you, and if you aren't

72

you, no one else can do. It seems to me that nature itself testifies to our uniqueness when it gives us such singular physical identity as fingerprints, footprints, elbow prints, and knee prints which are different from all others.

Even our voices, they say, have a print uniquely their own. It looks as if the Creator went to great trouble to give each of us individual marks of identification, so that no one could be considered the property of another. The New Testament underlines that idea in its teaching that each of us is of such ultimate, individual worth that God would present a plan for our salvation. The Spirit of God proves the point still further by dealing with us individually and specially.

So I'm convinced, on the basis of my Christian faith, that I've "gotta be me," and you have to be you. In fact, I feel that this is, above all else, a religious problem. True, it is a human problem and a psychological one. But even more, it is a religious problem. For Christianity is meant to set us free and to let us gain our true identity.

But if you looked carefully at the title of this sermon, you may have noticed that I concluded it not with an exclamation point or a period, but with a question mark. Mind you, I believe you must indeed be you. But here's what troubles me: when you say, "I've gotta be me," what *'me'* do you have in mind?

I'm thinking, for instance, of the person whose life seems shut in by what he calls fate, by prior decisions and by circumstances beyond his control. For such a person the cry, "I've gotta be me!" is not a shout of freedom but a cry of despair. That's the fear of his life—that he's sentenced to live forever in this prison house to which circumstances have banished him.

That's the sort of thing Saint Paul had in mind when he

73

described the state of a person lost in sin. "I do not understand my own actions," he wrote. "For I do not do what I want, but I do the very thing I hate. . . .Wretched man that I am! Who will deliver me from this body of death?"[2] It seemed to Paul that he was carrying a dead man around with him, and he wanted desperately to be free of his intolerable burden. Shall we say to such a person, "You have to be what you are"?

Obviously, he doesn't want to continue being what he is. He hopes that he can be something else. But the person who is deeply bogged in trouble is often convinced that this is his true state. I think, for instance, of the man who says, "I've got this miserable temperament. I make everyone around me unhappy. But I can't help myself. It's just the way I am. I've always been this way. How can you help what you *are*?" If you say to such a person, "You've gotta be you," he replies, "That's my whole trouble. I don't *want* to be me. I'd like to be delivered from this body of death."

So for some, "I've gotta be me" is a song of complaint. But even the man who thinks of it as a declaration of freedom may be selling life short. When he cries out, "I've gotta be me," he may have such a low estimate of himself that the cry is a limitation, though he knows it not. A person's estimate of himself is so very important. If a student judges that he is capable only of "C" work, he'll probably never rise above that level, even though he may actually be capable of excellent or superior work. That's why it's so important to know the potential of the real "me."

You should indeed be free, be yourself. But what is your true self? Is it possible that you have too low an estimate of yourself, and that your potential is far greater than you have ever

74

imagined?

The Bible has a high opinion of you and me. It's far higher than any political or economic system could ever dare to suggest. For instance, Saint John writes, "Now are we the sons of God, and it hath not yet appeared what we shall be . . ."[3] Great expectations! As Christians we are already the sons of God, and we have still greater prospects ahead. The Christian gospel sees the person—the *real* person—that is locked up inside us. Here's a man who seems inadequate and ineffective, and when he dares to cry, "I want to be me," he doesn't really hope for much! Any optimistic expectations make him sound like a Walter Mitty. But the Gospel sees the real potential of that man: adequate, strong, effective. He doesn't know what kind of "me" can be let loose. Even his best dreams are in dull gray, while God's redemption is a technicolor.

Jesus was constantly seeing potential in people which they could not see in themselves, and which their associates and peers did not see. Take that fisherman named Simon. I expect Simon would probably have sung this popular tune, "I've Gotta Be Me," with great enthusiasm. It seems that he was really himself—an unreconstructed character! A fisherman by trade, he was loud, robust, outspoken, and unpredictable. One moment he was a giant of a man, ready to die for his convictions, and the next he was like a whipped dog. Everyone knew what Simon was like, and so did Simon.

And then, one day he met Jesus. After a brief exchange Jesus said to him, "So you are Simon the son of John? You shall be called 'Rock.'" The author of the gospel was so impressed with this change of name that he reports Simon's new name in two languages, Aramaic and Greek. When the news spread that

Jesus had given Simon a new name, I wonder what his old friends said. "Simon a rock? Quicksilver maybe, or a pebble. But a *rock*? Huh!" And Simon must sometimes have said it to himself, especially on those occasions when he failed. On that night some time later when Simon denied his Lord three times—I wonder if he looked at his vacillating record and said, "That's the way I am . . . unstable as water. That's just the way I am." And I wonder if then he remembered: "But *He* called me *Peter*. He said I was a *Rock*." And Peter *was* a rock. Jesus had seen the man in Peter which he could not see in himself, and which none of his contemporaries could see.

That's what Jesus did with Zaccheus, too. Everyone knew what Zaccheus was, including especially Zaccheus: he was a money-grabber, a bit of a cheat, an unscrupulous traitor. But Jesus saw generosity in Zaccheus! Can you imagine that? He saw what Zaccheus *could* be, by the power of God. So, too, with Mary Magdalene. Every man in town knew what Mary was, and far too many of them were glad ot it. And *Mary* knew what she was. It sometimes seemed to her that she had known it all her life. She could remember, as a little girl, when older folks said, "Look at those eyes flash! You'll need to keep a tight rein on her." Before she reached her teens she heard men whisper, "Look at that girl. She's going to be a wild one." And wild she was, so wild that people said she had seven devils. But Jesus saw purity and virtue in her. He saw below the surface, beyond the obvious. He cut through reputation, history, yes even through fact, until He got down to the level *beneath* fact, the level of life out of which at last the facts are made. And down there, Jesus saw virtue, goodness, love: the woman Mary of Magdala was meant to be.

76

Nearly fifty years ago Trevor Davies said it this way. "The deepest, truest thing about the worst man is that he has been made in the image of God, and that, though it may be scarred and defaced, the divine impression can never be destroyed. . . . The conversion of such a man is actually a return to himself."[4]

You see, salvation is something more than "becoming religious." Salvation sets a person free. It gives him his first real chance to be himself—because it returns him to His proper Lord. "I gotta be me," we sing. True: but who is this *me*? Is it simply a wild grabbing for success? or an utterly undisciplined living? or a following of every passing impulse? What is your real, root "me"?

> Above all else, it is a person who was made, originally, in the image of God. And if you're really going to be you, the radical you, you must come back to that relationship and image. If you settle for being anything less, you've missed it.

Oh, I want you to be *you*. Not a slave to sin, not a compulsive seeker after pleasure, not a superficial success, not a well-trained brain or a slickly-tuned personality. I want you to be *you*, the fulfillment of what God meant you to be. God has such a wonderful plan for your life. He wants to set you *free*, to make you whole, to give you life. If you've been singing, "I've gotta be me," then come to the Lord who can bring it to pass. The possibilities are eternal.

It's so easy to forget what matters most . . .

If the Christian life could only be performed on paper or via a mathematical theorem, it would be so much easier to manage. Unfortunately, it has to be lived out in the daily run of work, weariness, irritation, and petty decisions. Furthermore, it is likely to be in the process of our little decisions that we will show most clearly where our affections lie. And it is likely to be the tiny irritations that, like a grain of sand in a great machine, may bring our spiritual development to a disappointing delay.

Most of all, we find it hard to keep our values straight. The immediate seems so important, while the larger, farther good slips out of focus. At such times, we sometimes become ashamed of our best.

Ashamed of Our Best

You can often measure the true quality of a human being by what he or she is proud of. You can also measure it by what a person is *ashamed of*.

Simon Peter was ashamed of the best thing that ever came into his life. There was so much in Peter's life of which he had reason to be ashamed; in this he was like most of us. He ought well to have been ashamed of his temper, his coarse, Vesuvius-like temper. And his fumbling vacillation—that deserved shame. Probably, too, he had reason to be ashamed of his past; and in the early days of his discipleship he might well have been ashamed of the slight measure of his accomplishments.

> But instead, he was ashamed of his best; of the one good, honorable, and blessed fact of his life.
> And so often, you and I are like him. We are pathetically, embarrassingly like him. We are ashamed of our best.

You remember Peter's story. He was a loud, roustabout fisherman when Jesus came into his life. But soon the mercurial fisherman was part of the most important dozen men who ever joined forces for good. For some three years, he lived within arm's length of the Master, hearing His teaching, helping Him in the healing of the sick, feeling the thunder of heaven in his soul. He became one of the inner circle of three who were nearest to Jesus, and in many instances served as spokesman for the group.

Then the day came when they brought Jesus to trial, and it was clear that they would crucify Him. As Peter stood off at the edge of the gathering, some people in the crowd thought they recognized him as a follower of the Nazarene.

Now suppose *you* had walked with Jesus: suppose He had chosen you as one of His twelve, and you had been with Him in the healing and teaching and mending of life. You would know, wouldn't you, that this was the best thing in your life, this association with Christ? And if someone in the crowd had said, "Do you know this Jesus?" wouldn't you have wanted to say, "You bet your life I know Him! I've lived with Him and worked with Him, and I'm one of His team. He's the proudest fact of my life!"

That's what you'd want to say, isn't it? Shouldn't a person be proud of his best? Shouldn't he glory, if he would glory in anything, in the one good, honorable, and blessed fact of his life?

Well, it wasn't that way with Peter. "I'll be damned," he said, I'll be damned if I ever knew Him!" Simon Peter was *ashamed of his best*. He was ashamed of the one thing in his life of which he had reason to be proud.

And so often we are like him. So often we are ashamed of our best.

Take the matter of our Christian *faith*. We will talk freely of our affection for a certain make of automobile or a brand of cosmetics; we will even talk freely of our political allegiance—and then we will grow silent regarding our faith. Let me be very clear: We may even talk rather freely about our church—its

82

choir, its social occasions, its ministers—but we're ashamed to talk about our *faith*, the deep, God-touched spot in our lives.

"That's personal," someone replies. Indeed! How poor we would be if Charles Wesley had taken that attitude about his faith, and had never shared it with us in his hymns. "Where shall my wondering soul begin?" Wesley asked. How could he recount the story of God's grace? It was such a personal story, so that Wesley's hymns are full of pronouns in the first person singular. He might have argued that he should keep such reflections to himself. To our eternal good fortune, he shared what he was experiencing. So, too, with the writers of the Psalms, and the prophets. How poor we would be if they had clutched their struggles and victories to themselves as "too personal to tell."

And for that matter, how cheated we would be if Peter had chosen to keep the story of our text to himself. Surely nothing that happened to Peter was more personal than this hour of his denial. No doubt the knowledge of that denial would never have been preserved if Peter himself had not shared it with others. We can be glad that the Peter who once was ashamed of his faith ultimately had the courage to declare the goodness of God, even though it was at the cost of confessing his own failure.

On those occasions when I use public transportation, I delight in the opportunity to do a little reading. Usually that reading is in the nature of a magazine or a newspaper or perhaps a light novel. Some time ago, however, I felt like reading my Bible; a particular passage was very much on my mind, and I wanted to look at it. But I hesitated: what will people think of me, I asked myself, if they see me reading a Bible on the bus?

83

Now isn't that astonishing? The Bible is the best book in my life: it is by every measure the finest thing I read. How astonishing that I should feel self-conscious about reading the Bible in public—ashamed of my best!

Now of course my hesitancy was not all bad. One reason that some of us draw back from such an act as reading our Bible in public is because we don't want to be guilty of a display of piety; a public show of religion seems Pharisaical. Goodness knows I wouldn't want to become this kind of person, nor do I like to see people parading their religion. But neither would I want us to be embarrassed by our faith. Why should a person apologize for wanting to read his Bible? If we can read a popular magazine, a novel, or a textbook while riding the bus, why not the Bible—without apology or superiority. Why be ashamed of our best?

Not only are we sometimes ashamed of our faith, but also of our best *convictions*. So often we give the impression of being less than we are. A young person happens, for example, to love good music; here is something to be proud of. Instead, he will act as if he prefers the shoddy, the cheap, the transient. He is ashamed of his best. And sometimes a young person, in high school or on a college campus, is overwhelmed by a loud, crude minority. You have been taught to be neat, clean, and groomed, but you allow yourself to be intimidated by the idea that it may be clever to be slovenly and ill-kempt. Why be ashamed of your best?

This embarrassment over our best convictions is especially characteristic of our feeling about drinking. I have heard people boast about how drunk they have gotten, with the perverse

84

notion that this was something of an achievement, and by inexplainable contrast, I have known numbers of people who were ashamed that they do *not* drink—as if being a teetotaler were a cause of social embarrassment! Some of you know what I mean: the kind of person who doesn't drink (whether out of conviction or simply out of personal taste) but who will accept a cocktail at a party and carry it around all evening, to give the impression of drinking. Or perhaps still worse, that person who takes several drinks in the evening and pours them, in a private moment, on a potted palm—thus complicating his shame by a crime against the floral kingdom.

> Why be ashamed that you don't drink? Why be ashamed that you are making no contribution to a business that finds 200,000 new victims each year? Why be ashamed that you are different: and different—at that—on the safe and productive side? Why be ashamed of your *best*? Whatever one might say about drinking, he would hardly say that it is the *best* way—why, then, be ashamed of the best?

Another thing. In certain settings—in a group of men at work, or in a bull session in the fraternity house, or perhaps a group of girls in a dormitory conversation—sexual promiscuity becomes a matter of pride, and virginity is made to seem unknowing. For most of us, sexual purity is not easily come by; why should anyone feel embarassed that he has no sexual misadventures to report to the bull session or the dormitory gabfest? Why should we be ashamed of our best?

Our *nation*, too, has come to be ashamed of its best. We have maligned such words as *pious* and *Puritan*. We discredit a style of life which gave a foundation to our nation and its commitments to liberty. "Puritan" has become a dirty word among intellectuals and newspaper writers—including many who don't know enough history to evaluate the term. I would not suggest that the Puritans were a perfect people. Like most of us, they found it hard to keep life in balance. But their commitment to conscience and liberty, and their readiness to examine their own souls and to seek purity of life and worship are qualities we would do well to re-claim today.

And have you considered how often we are ashamed of our *heart*, of the tender quality in human nature? When is a person at his or her best? When he is crude and cruel and coarse? is this the height of our humanity? Some people seem to think so. Isn't it really too bad that we should be ashamed to be polite, or tender, or that we should be afraid to use terms of endearment? Isn't it astonishing that people find it easier to say 'damn' than to say 'dear' or 'thank you'?

I am ashamed of the generation in which I live because so many of us feel obligated, in this pseudo-sophisticated twentieth century world, to preface or postlogue every deep expression of feeling with the statement, "I know this sounds corny, but..." Why can't we confess a human—a *humane*—feeling, a valid, authentic, heart-deep, human feeling without a sense of shame or embarrassment for having such a feeling? The ancient Hebrews, the English of Shakespeare's day, and quite a few people in our own day, have learned that a human being is more of a human being when his face can register tears, compassion, and sentiment, than when it is a 'sophisticated,' empty, asinine mask. How astonishing that we should be ashamed of our *best,* our *heart*! How unbelievable that we

86

should think more of hardness than of tenderness! Don't we confess how weak and inadequate we really are when we insist on wearing a mask? If we were *really* strong, we would dare to have feelings, and to let them be known.

What do we confess about ourselves when we seem to be ashamed of our best? What are we saying about our true sense of values? or, perhaps, what are we confessing about our fear of people? Is it true, as it appears, that we are more concerned with what others think than we are with what God thinks, or with what we must confess to our own souls?

I am not asking us to stand on the street corner, announcing our beliefs. Nor am I suggesting that we intrude religion upon every conversation; to do so, in fact, would sometimes work more harm than good. But I *am* saying that goodness is nothing to be ashamed of—and that when someone asks, "Do you know Him?" as they long ago asked Peter, we should answer, proudly, "Yes—He is the best fact of my life."

Someone *will* ask you that question tomorrow, I venture; someone usually asks the question every day. We often miss the question, because it is not asked directly. It is clothed in the garb of daily life.

And this is exactly as it ought to be and as we ought to have expected, because Christianity has no other domain than the common day. The question comes at the lunch counter, at the office coffee break, in the classroom, or the street corner conversation. It comes as a statement about politics or ethics, morals or idle chit-chat; but when you are sensitive, you can hear behind the common speech the voice of a Palestinian

87

maiden asking, "Dost thou not know Him? I thought I saw thee walking with Him."

And afraid of the consequences of being Christian—afraid it will hurt our business or our social life or our ego—we stand on Peter's ancient ground: "I never knew Him." Usually, for us, it is an easy statement: we are simply silent when we ought to speak, or we are blase when we ought to be impassioned. "I never knew Him," we say.

And we are ashamed of our best. Ashamed of the one good, honorable, and blessed fact of our poor lives.

A word to mothers and fathers . . .

Being a parent has always been a complicated, challenging task, but in recent years some have decided that it is an almost impossible one. A mother or father might rightly say, as Saint Paul did in another setting, "Who is sufficient for these things?"

Sermons for Mother's Day or Father's Day are likely to relate to only a minority in the congregation. This sermon attempts to reach beyond those with children in the home and to challenge each of us to realize the degree to which we may be influencing the next generation.

Books That Babies Can Read

Some years ago a young man was brought to trial for a serious crime. As the full shame of his deed was made public and the judge prepared to pass sentence, the boy's mother was given opportunity to speak. In her grief she spoke hesitantly, trying to understand what had happened to her son.

"I just can't explain it," she said. "We always tried to give him every advantage, every opportunity. We provided him with a good education. We gave him the best books and magazines to read."

As far as the mother could see, she was right; and in the light of her interpretation of matters, she deserved empathy and even praise. But she was also wrong. No doubt she had given her son good books, perhaps the best of the past and the present. But she was too late in giving them.

What we need most if we are to change the pattern of our world is to provide good books for babies to read. There is only limited hope in giving a twelve-year-old *Gentlemen's Agreement* or a biography of George Washington Carver if he learned to say "nigger" and "kike" before he was seven. You'll have to argue eloquently to persuade a sixteen-year-old to remain chaste unless she read books that convinced her when she was three or four. It's difficult to prepare a twenty-year-old for happy marriage and parenthood if he wasn't reading the right books before he enrolled in kindergarten.

"But what books can be given to infants?" someone asks. "Babies can't read."

Ah, but they can, and they do. I venture that the books babies read before they are enrolled in school are probably the most important books that will ever çome into their lives. I am speaking of those things which children read in the lives of the people around them. The book of human conduct: there is no other quite like it. The print is large, the lessons are both clear and subtle, the illustrations command attention. Long before a child knows the alphabet, it has begun formulating profound and perhaps lifelong attitudes about God, character, love, and human values. The infant may not be able to verbalize those ideas until years later—in fact, some of the ideas may always be a little beyond verbalization; perhaps that's why we sometimes say, "I don't really know why I feel the way I do"—but the ideas are there. A baby has read them in the most persuasive of all books, the conduct of those around her.

How important are the books babies can read? Many marriage counsellors now insist that the average person's attitude toward marriage is settled by the time he is six years old. That means the literature of parental conduct is terribly effective, for good or ill. A sociologist writes, "The family contacts with the child begin so early and during the all-important first three or four years of life are so exclusive and absorbing that nothing which occurs later can equal them in importance. . . . The family remains the real architect; it lays down the basic plan of the personality." Some psychiatrists feel they can trace the roots of certain forms of schizophrenia to the first weeks of infancy. Dr. O. Spurgeon English and Dr. Gerald Pearson put it quite simply: "The newborn child is a newcomer into the world and whatever attitude he meets in his environment he is likely to adopt and to carry throughout his life to a large degree."[1]

Sometimes, however, we folks at the workaday level of life are skeptical of the experts and their theories. If so, let me tell you some experiences from life—stories you no doubt can duplicate from your own experience. For example, there's the forty-year-old woman—basically moral, religious, and conscientious—who told me why she isn't a church member. "I think I made up my mind before I was out of first grade that I'd never go to church if I had my own way. I was already sick of seeing my mother lose her temper in the rush of preparing the family for Sunday School, then go to church and sing as if she were a saint." That isn't really a very thoughtful analysis, but it comes from the kind of books that babies can read.

Or I think of a conversation with a pregnant, unmarried teenager. As we counselled, I asked how her parents felt about her circumstances, and she replied, "What does it matter how they feel? Where do you think I got my twisted ideas about sex?" Her statement wasn't adequate, for none of us really has the right to blame his actions on someone else. Nevertheless, she was reporting how she felt. And though she wouldn't have put it that way, she was simply demonstrating that some books which babies read make so deep an impression that teenage sex education classes may never quite replace them.

Now I hasten to say, and to say emphatically, that I believe in the power of God to redeem human life. I am a minister of the Gospel because I believe lost souls can be restored, shattered lives rebuilt, wrecked homes reestablished. If I didn't believe so, I'm not sure I'd have the courage to face each day's work. But because I've seen so much of broken lives, I know the importance of bringing God into life before it is already badly

93

damaged. It is magnificent to see God transform an alcoholic, but it is better to see a child raised with such a faith that he never loses years of his life in alcoholism. And of course the same point can be made with drugs, illegitimacy, or imprisonment: I know God can redeem such lives, and I have seen Him do so. I rejoice in such transformations. But it would be better, surely, if we could raise children in such a way that they would be spared the anguish of lost years and scarred character.

That's why I appeal this Mother's Day for good books for babies to read. Medical science, psychoanalysts, and sociologists all contend that the first half-dozen years of a child's life are by far the most important in the shaping of character and personality. Yet a child is not enrolled in school until he is past five; he does not usually learn to read until he is six or more; and we ministers do not receive him for confirmation training until he is twelve or thirteen.

Before a child can read with his eyes and his brain, he begins to read with his emotions, his heart, his feelings. We do not yet fully understand the meaning of those inherent powers which we call "instinct," yet we have learned that as surely as we are human, a baby can tell when it is loved and wanted. Babies read the book of human emotions—love and hatred, fear and joy, faith and doubt, terror and security. Sometimes, in fact, it seems as if an infant—or even a household pet—is more sensitive to these emotional "soundwaves" than are we adults.

The Old Testament carries a warning which at first is offensive because it seems unfair. It declares that God is a jealous God who visits the "iniquity of the fathers upon the children to the third and fourth generation"[2] of those who hate Him. These harsh words, it seems to me, are not so much a

94

divine curse as a straightforward declaration of the way life is. No generation lives and dies to itself. We are bound to the past by cords of heredity, psychology, and influence. If the generations just before us have been possessed of hate, fear, and vindictiveness, we will suffer some of the penalty. Only by great effort will we be able to escape reaping the harvest which our parents and grandparents have sown. And so much of this influence comes, the psychologist tells us, not in direct teaching but in unconscious influence; and it comes in some of the earliest years of infancy, during the period when babies read the books of human conduct.

I hope you understand that while I preach this sermon on Mother's Day, it isn't intended simply for mothers. Obviously it applies almost as much to fathers; for while they may not spend as much time with an infant as the mother, they have the same emotional potential for communication. It is also a sermon for every babysitter. I wonder if a babysitter knows how great her influence may be? or if parents anticipate the good or harm a sitter may do, depending on her own emotional health?

But this is a sermon, really, for every one of us who ever touches the life of a child. If we pause to delve into the past, each of us will recall neighbors, relatives, and friends of our parents who made an impression upon us when we were six or seven years old; these are the experiences available to conscious memory. But this is only the tip of the iceberg. Our unconscious memory must have an almost unbelievable store of persons and experiences: a hearty laugh, a gruff voice, a gentle touch, a quiet assurance, a sense of caring, a coldness or an indifference.

Say to yourself, then, when you come to a place where there

95

are infants and little children, "I am feeding something into the data bank of this human life. I'll never know how much impression I make; but I must remember that the human personality is the most impressionable of all material, and that I will inevitably be something of a contributor to this child's future temperament and character. I will try, therefore, to bring beauty and loveliness into this life."

But this rule of life is too significant to be limited simply to our relationships with children. What about our influence upon the personalities of young people and adults? Mind you, I think that most of us in the youth and adult age groups are not quite so sensitive to human conduct as are children. This is because we have so many distractions and preoccupations. As far as we know, an infant perceives life only through the influence of human personality; this is virtually the only "book" which they read, except for the book of their natural surroundings. We adults are involved with a very maze of demands and influences.

Nevertheless, even we adults are more influenced by the attitudes and manners of other people than we fully realize. Have you noticed, for instance, that sometimes you feel either good or distressed for no particular reason? I don't think any of our feelings are really without reason; it's only that we don't understand or discern the reason. I wonder how often our unexplained elation or distress is a result of a passing smile or a passing frown, a pleasant greeting or a harsh rebuke, a gracious clerk or a grumpy customer. I wonder how much of the color of our daily lives comes from the fleeting experiences of passing human relationships? Not simply the potentially powerful impressions from the members of our families; sometimes we build up a defense or an immunity against these continuing influences. But what about the fragile, tiny, apparently inconsequential experiences? what kind of mosaic of impression do they make in our lives? Even though we adults are reading so many more "books" than the babies read, yet we too are constantly influenced by our contacts with human personality and conduct.

If that be so—if we human beings are so much touched by other lives—then what manner of persons ought we to be in our daily walk? When it is in our power to tilt the scale of life toward joy or pain for other people, shouldn't we pray for the grace to be a constant influence for goodness and beauty?

From an academic point of view, we are the most psychologically informed generation in human history. We know that a person's attitude toward life is so largely shaped during the first five or six years of life; we know that there are settings in which mental health is fostered, while in other circumstances it is corrupted. But with all that we know, the world will not be a greatly better place in which to live unless we have the will to make it better. Specifically, unless we choose to cast our weight on the side of what is good.

To put it in the language of our sermon title: the infants in our world get their personality and character and attitude toward life almost entirely from books that babies can read—the books of human relationship, whether mother, father, baby sitter, or passing stranger. And the youth and adult world still gets a surprising amount of its emotional input from the same source. In such a world as this, each one of us should know that he is

97

constantly writing a book—one that is widely read. May God help us to add volumes to the library of life that will communicate faith, love, hope, joy, and peace to all our readers.

Thoughts upon entering a polling booth . . .

The apostle Paul once said that he was "a citizen of no mean city," and on other occasions he used his Roman citizenship to good purpose. If Paul could feel that kind of pride in his citizenship in an empire, how much more pride and responsibility ought a Christian to feel when he or she lives in a democratic republic?

But what do we do with our citizenship when at last we pull the curtains on the polling booth and find ourselves alone with God and our choices? And what do we do about our citizenship prior to that sacred moment, in the weeks when we're listening to campaign speeches and television commercials? And (still more challenging)—ought some of us sometime be willing to become candidates or active campaigners for candidates?

When the Trees Held an Election

In this good land of ours where we seem always to be holding some sort of election, it is appropriate that we pause for a few moments to recall the time when the trees held an election. We Americans have a love affair with the ballot box. Mind you, we turn out an improperly small percentage of voters for each election, but perhaps this is at least partly because we insist on having a voice in selecting so many public officials: school board members, judges, county clerks, mayors, council members, state legislators, governors, congressmen, senators, and presidents. And in that list, I have touched only the more obvious offices. Voting is a lively subject for us, and it ought to be. So what political lesson can the trees teach us?

You will find the story in the Old Testament book of Judges, chapter nine. The ancient nation of Israel had enjoyed triumph and prosperity under an able judge named Gideon. As the Scripture puts it, "The land had rest forty years in the days of Gideon."[1] But when he died, there was no effective leader to take his place. It is rather a common experience in both nations and political parties that the death or retirement of a great leader reveal that there's no one really ready to fill the void. In this instance, the nation turned quite naturally to Gideon's own family. The potential seemed to be there, for Gideon had a total of seventy sons by his several wives. I don't know if any of the seventy were qualified. At any rate, no one stepped out of the ranks quickly enough. Instead, another son who had been born to one of Gideon's maidservants organized a small political revolt and murdered all of the seventy recognized sons.

All, that is, except one. One named Jotham managed to escape. When his illegitimate half-brother was crowned, Jotham stood on top of Mount Gerizim and made a speech. It was a parable, and no one in the crowd could have missed its point:

> The trees once went forth to anoint a king over them; and they said to the olive tree, 'Reign over us.' But the olive tree said to them, 'Shall I leave my fatness, by which gods and men are honored, and go to sway over the trees?' And the trees said to the fig tree, 'Come you, and reign over us.' But the fig tree said to them, 'Shall I leave my sweetness and my good fruit, and go to sway over the trees?' And the trees said to the vine, 'Come you, and reign over us.' But the vine said to them, 'Shall I leave my vine which cheers gods and men, and go to sway over the trees?' Then all the trees said to the bramble, 'Come you, and reign over us.' And the bramble said to the trees, 'If in good faith you are anointing me king over you, then come and take refuge in my shade; but if not, let fire come out of the bramble and devour the cedars of Lebanon.'[2]

What Jotham said centuries ago about the political situation in his land seems uncomfortably appropriate to our own day. The trees were agreed that they needed a ruler, and they were wise enough to know that it ought to be a great ruler. They therefore set out to get the most notable of their company, a figure that would command the respect of all the forest. Their first choice, therefore, was the olive tree. Everybody in Jotham's audience could understand such a choice. The olive tree was the most important plant in ancient Israel. It affected nearly every aspect of daily life, by providing food, fuel, light, carpentry, ointments, and medicine. Furthermore, its cultivation was simple, and it would grow even in the rocky soil of that rugged land, bearing fruit biennially for hundreds of years. Early Mesopotamian art sometimes portrayed the olive as the tree of life.[3]

But when the olive tree was asked if he would accept nomination and election, he replied with disdain, "Shall I leave my fatness . . . and go sway over the trees?" The language is instructive. The word "fatness" suggests the productiveness and worthwhileness of his present post; and when he speaks of going to "sway" over the trees, one's mind pictures idle grandeur and display, a kind of meaningless pomposity.

The delegation then approached the fig tree, which was prized by ancient peoples not only because it gave food but also for the pleasure which its food provided. But the fig tree replied, "Shall I leave my sweetness and my good fruit . . . and go to sway over the trees?" So they went to the vine. It wasn't as impressive as the others, but because the grape was crucial to the lives of the people, the vine was held in regard. But the vine answered as had the olive and the fig: why leave his fruitfulness to sway over the trees?

Then, in desperation, the trees approached the bramble. The bramble was useless and ugly. It could not even cast sufficient shadow to give comfort to a weary traveler. It was usually a tangled mass of sharp spines and runners. How absurd to think of the bramble sitting in the seat of authority over the olive tree, the Cedar of Lebanon, or the majestic oak! But the trees asked the bramble, as Jotham told the story, and the bramble

103

answered, "I'll do it, if you'll come and take refuge in my shade . . ."

We understand Jotham's parable. A century ago, when the Tweed-Croker political machine was running New York City, Josiah Gilbert Holland wrote a prayer fitting of a prophet:

> God, give us Men! A time like this demands
> Strong minds, great hearts, true faith and ready hands;
>   Men whom the lust of office does not kill;
> Men whom the spoils of office cannot buy;
>   Men who possess opinions and a will;
> Men who have honor; men who will not lie;
> Men who can stand before a demogogue
>   And damn his treacherous flatteries without winking!
> Tall men, sun-crowned . . .

That indeed is what we seek: "tall men, sun-crowned"—a veritable oak, or redwood; and instead, all too often, we come up with a bramble.

Now there's a frightening irony in the bramble. It isn't simply that it's thorny, useless, and absurd. Professor Jacob M. Myers reminds us that a bramble may harbor and spread a fire which can destroy even the great cedars of the forest.[4] If inadequate leadership were only a neutral factor in the affairs of earth, we might conceivably endure it; but as the parable suggests, it may be far worse: it may become the carrier of the raging, irrational fires of destruction. As Barbara Tuchman, the popular interpreter of history, puts it, "In public affairs, stupidity is more dangerous than knavery."[5]

A dozen years ago, in another election year, TIME magazine dedicated its weekly "essay" to the hunger for a true leader.

"The age cries out for greatness in the White House," the essay said. It made no attempt to evaluate the candidates then on the scene; it didn't even mention their names or hint by description. But as it analyzed the awesome responsibilities of the American presidency it declared that what voters should more than ever seek was that "most obvious and most elusive" quality, *character*. "Americans *want* their President to be great," the Essay said, "or at least admirable. For all the dissent and despair, Americans are not yet cynical, and have not yet lost their capacity for enthusiasm."[6]

That sentence worries me. It may have been true then that our people were not yet cynical and had not yet lost their capacity for enthusiasm, but I'm not sure it is so today. I sense so much apathy in the American electorate as we approach another national election. And with reason. Some time ago, as presidential primaries began and we had the choice of a dozen or fifteen declared candidates, I had the feeling that there may never have been a time when we had so many likely candidates for the vice-presidency; but was there a *president* in the group?

Mind you, a vice-president ought to be as potentially great as the president, since he is only a heartbeat away from the office, but we have traditionally chosen rather bland, inoffensive vice-presidents, people meant to offer geographical or strategic balance to the ticket. In recent times, it seems to me, that's mainly what we've been offered; a kind of bland balance. A bland balance to blandness, verily. Our hearts and minds cry for an oak, an olive, or a cedar of Lebanon, and we're offered a bramble.

In his parable Jotham included a bitterly ironic line. When the bramble was finally nominated, it said, "I accept, if you'll

105

take refuge in my shade. . ." What shade could one find in a bramble? How long would one have to stoop in order to find refuge in that poor, thorny thing? So these days, when candidates cry, "Vote for me," one sometimes wants to ask, "Could there possibly be any shade in *that*?"

It has not always been so bleak. The miracle of our American story lies in the extraordinary collection of leaders which came to the fore in the time of the American Revolution. It is almost unbelievable that one small nation could in one brief period produce a Franklin, a Washington, a Jefferson, a Madison, Sam and John Adams, and half-a-dozen other giants.

No, let me correct that statement. It isn't surprising that we had such men, but it is surprising that we had them in *public service*. I believe that every generation of American history has men and women somewhat comparable to those great heroes. But in too many instances they say, like the olive or the fig tree, "Why should I leave my fatness and my sweetness to 'sway over the trees'?" Or translated, "Why should I leave my business or profession, with its security, to dirty my hands in politics?"

Now then, if you wonder why sometimes the bramble is ruling over the oaks and the cedars, you can blame it on the oaks and cedars and olive trees that refused to leave their frutiful posts because they saw government as little more than swaying grandly over the trees. Jotham's parable makes fun of the bramble, but its point of anger is toward the trees of the forest that caused the bramble to take on such unlikely significance.

Several years ago I spent the better part of a morning visiting with a businessman and his pastor in a southern state. The businessman was a dedicated Christian with a humanness and a breadth of ability that our political offices need. His pastor told

106

me that he had urged him into politics for several years, until at last he had run for a county post. He was elected, and served well. But he said that the most difficult part of the whole experience came each time he campaigned in shopping centers. Potential voters would so often say, "Well you must be a crook or you wouldn't be running for office." No wonder the trees sometimes get a bramble to rule over them!

The media also play a part. We want them to be watchdogs, a true fourth estate. But one often feels that when they get short on news, they turn to the kind of nit-picking and snide innuendos which have more to do with back fence gossip than with responsible investigation. What honorable person wants to subject himself or herself to such treatment?

Our minds have become conditioned to an unhealthy attitude toward politics. Some years ago I visited for several hours with a brilliant young African as we flew from Addis Ababa, Ethiopia, to Nairobi, Kenya. When I looked at his passport, I discovered that the line asking "occupation" bore the answer, "politician." I told my new friend, Josiah Kariuki, that it seemed a strange answer, because for so many of us 'politician' is a dirty word. But not to this young African. He had gone to college to prepare for a career in government. He had just spent several years in a detention camp to pay for his convictions. Now his country was soon to become independent, and he intended to dedicate his learning, his ability, and his energy to political leadership.

In ancient Israel, government was not looked upon as dirty business. Instead, it was assumed that the judge or the general or the king should be a servant of God. The Bible mentions priest, prophet, and king in the same breath, considering them all to be God's ministers.

107

The king was ordained to his task with holy anointing oil, just as was a priest or a prophet. Some of those kings failed, but the Jewish people continued to have a sense of divine regard for the throne. They expected greatness from their rulers because they believed God had a stake in government.

I mentioned a few moments ago that America had extraordinary leadership at the time of the American Revolution. I'm sure that at least part of the reason can be found in the Colonial practice of the Election Day Sermons. Those early Americans were constantly reminded, by the pulpit, that government is a divine responsibility. We need a re-birth of that thinking today. I don't really care which party you choose for your efforts. I'm satisfied, from what I know of history and current events, that neither major party has a monopoly on either heroes or scoundrels. But I think it is time—indeed, past time!—to recognize that the political process is not demonic. To the contrary, it has the capacity to be divine. And it is time to confess that if the trees are ruled over by brambles, you can't blame the brambles. They're simply filling a void. Blame the olives, the figs, and the vines who won't accept responsibility. And blame all the trees of the forest that discourage the great trees from taking leadership.

And remember that our times, like all previous times and more than most, cry for great human beings: people of intelligence, ability, and above all else, character. If we aren't getting enough persons of this stature in government, we ought to begin turning the tide. For eventually, inevitably, we get the leaders we deserve: brambles, or cedars of Lebanon.

What do you do with Thanksgiving Day? . . .

Most of us sense that we have reason to be thankful, though probably we don't realize it often enough. But at Thanksgiving time, the season conspires with our own sense of gratitude, and we want to express our thanks.

But how shall we go about it? What are the matters for which we ought to be thankful, and how do we say it? "Thank you" seems so inadequate when you begin to total up your blessings, or as many of your blessings as you can recognize. And that's another problem: how do we develop the faith and the sensitivity of spirit to know our blessings when we see them?

Here's a word for Thanksgiving week, or for any day of any week. After all, gratitude is never out of season.

A Bread and Butter Note to God

"The Little Locksmith" is a remarkable book, but the reason why it was written is even more remarkable.

The book is the autobiography of Katharine Butler Hathaway, a tiny lady whose life story was almost entirely an internal affair. She was elected to no offices, won no championships, amassed no fortune. She had no hair-raising adventures, no trips to exotic lands, no affairs to be reported by a gossip columnist. As a child of five she contracted tuberculosis of the spine. She spent the next ten years of her life, twenty-four hours of every day, strapped to a hard, sloping bed, with a leather halter under her chin to hold her head erect. In spite of all these efforts, however, when she was finally released from her little prison, at age fifteen, she was a hunchback.

So as a mature woman she wrote her life's story. It was, of course, primarily a record of the thoughts that went through her mind in a lifetime of physical limitations. It is a strange and beautiful book, and not at all sad, though in synopsis it would seem that it would have to be.

But the most remarkable thing about the book, as I said a moment ago, was the reason for which it was written. She explains it in an epilogue:

> I first began to tell my story because I needed to express my thanks for the things that have happened to me. In the beginning I said to someone, this book is going to be my bread-and-butter letter to God.[1]

111

As I read Miss Hathaway's statement I thought immediately, that's what the Thanksgiving holiday should be: a bread-and-butter letter to God.

So I looked into the old classic of good manners, Emily Post's *Etiquette.* "When you have been staying over a Sunday, or for longer, in someone's house," Miss Post wrote, "it is absolutely necessary that you write a letter of thanks to your hostess within a few days after the visit."[2] If that's the standard for a bread-and-butter letter, there's no question but what it's appropriate for us to address such a communication to God. We've been staying in His house not simply for a weekend, but for a lifetime. The earth is His, and He made it. How could I live here year after year without taking time, again and again, to offer an expression of thanks?

Emily Post says that bread and butter letters are stumbling-blocks for almost everyone. People find them very hard to do, probably because they are often written to persons with whom one is on formal terms, while the letter itself should be somewhat informal in tone. Perhaps that's part of our problem in Thanksgiving. The very act of thanks ought to have a certain warmth and intimacy about it, and great numbers of people just don't feel they know God that well. Thanksgiving therefore becomes an uncomfortable formality; we don't know how to begin, develop or end the letter. It's frustrating to have a warm feeling of gratitude and not be able to communicate it. So like many a poor guest, we postpone our word of thanks until at last we feel guilty about it; and then the thanks becomes so colored with uneasiness that it loses all its original quality of gratitude until we may even forget it altogether.

But there may be a deeper reason why we've neglected our

bread and butter note to God. Katharine Butler Hathway wrote, "We fell in love with ourselves and our works, and forgot our manners." She observes that we became more and more greedy and harder to please, until we were "arrogant, ill-bred guests" taking what we wanted and forgetting to "guard our happiness with humility and prayer."[3]

If this was true in 1942, when it was originally written, I fear it is even more true today. We have lived with nearly thirty years of prosperity since the end of World War II, and we have surrounded ourselves with mechanical conveniences—some of them wonderfully practical and worthwhile and some of them shamefully absurd. But strangely enough, our abundance hasn't made us more thankful. In many instances, we've simply become more demanding. The truth is, it's very hard to live with abundance without coming to feel that abundance is your right; until at last you hardly think to thank your Host.

Yet some people have retained their spirit of gratitude, even in the midst of an often unthankful world. This gratitude comes when we remember that we are *guests*. This world is not our possession. We live here only temporarily. It was waiting for us when we moved into our particular guest chamber, and it will still be here when we move on and someone else takes over our spot. If we remember that we are guests, we will begin to feel the beautiful joy of thanksgiving, and we'll be anxious to address our bread and butter note to God.

Now what should such a letter say? First, thanks for *hospitality* enjoyed. This is the mood I find everywhere in the Book of Psalms. I think for example of a verse in Psalm 4: "Thou hast given me room when I was in distress."[4] That's the kind of hospitality God has extended to every one of us. When you're in distress, it's almost as if life itself has evicted you. Where can you stay? Some of your former residences no longer seem adequate. I'm thinking of such a time as a period of serious illness, or a crisis in your marriage or romance, or the apparent failure of some important friendship. Now the house of financial security or psychological adjustment or courageous optimism seems insignificant. At such times we turn to God with new abandon, and He provides us *room*. How wonderful to have a place to stay when you are in distress! At a time when you may be unwelcome in most places, God is a host who will take you in.

When I think of the hospitality of God, I also recall a phrase which appears at least three times in the Book of Psalms: "(Thou) has not shut me up into the hand of the enemy; thou hast set my feet in a large room."[5] I'm thankful to my Host that He has so often given me a *large* room! He has provided me not simply with the necessities of life, a bare subsistence, a six-by-eight cell, but He has surrounded me with blessings.

When the term "bread and butter letter" first came into common use, it was quite accurate. People lived very modestly, and if they entertained someone for overnight, the food provided was likely to be little more than bread, butter, beverage, and soup. Yet we still use the phrase today, when a guest receives not only bread and butter, but meat and vegetables and dessert, bedroom, living room, television set, and probably dinner in a restaurant or attendance at a cultural or sporting event. So, too, in much of our experience with God. He has given us not simply bread and butter, but a list of benefits beyond our enumerating. In unhappy days we sometimes think everything has gone wrong; but when we stop

114

long enough to study our surroundings—that is, to think life through—we realize that God has put us in "a large room." His divine hospitality is beautiful to behold.

Some of us can remember youthful days when any bread-and-butter note to a hostess inevitably included a list of apologies. With adolescent thoughtlessness, we had been noisy too late at night; in our growing awkwardness we had bumped against a lamp and bent a shade; or perhaps we had returned so late at night that we had kept our hostess awake beyond her usual hours. Apologies were in order.

Our bread and butter note to God ought to include the same element. We have been given so much, and so often we have abused the hospitality which heaven has extended to us. There is the ultimate gift of life itself: we waste so much of it, sometimes because we're waiting for tomorrow and thus losing today, sometimes because we're bored—what a sad thing to say about life!— and sometimes because we're spending the time in hating, resenting, or coveting. And our good body: very few of us would treat an automobile or a stereo the way we treat our irreplaceable body. Any bread and butter note to our Divine Host calls for an apology for the misuse of our bodies. And the rest of the list each of us should compile for himself: a voice to sing, a mind to learn, a heart to love, a hand to lift, a book to read, a world to behold: how much of it, dear Host, have we returned to you slightly bent or broken?

Most of all, I expect, our bread and butter note should acknowledge that all the favors we have received are undeserved. "I made it with my own hand," we say. "Look at what I've accomplished." And the voice asks, "*Whose* hand? Who said it was yours? Where did you get the talent, the flash of insight, the perseverance to achieve?" Or we speak of our moral worth. "I've been good, you know." But suddenly we realize the absurdity of declaring our goodness before the perfect One. Slowly, slowly it dawns on us that we can never repay our Host, never deserve the benefits we have received. The best we can do is to be a reasonably grateful guest.

No, no; we can do more than that. We can do a truly right and noble thing. Katharine Butler Hathaway wrote a book as her bread and butter letter to God, and in doing so she blessed the lives of many thousands of persons. But of course the book was only a verbalization of the life she had already lived for Him.

And this is what *we* can do. Since we have enjoyed God's immense hospitality in this His world, we can open our hearts and welcome Him into the only home we have to offer: a loving heart. Remarkably, it is the home He most desires. In some profound sense, He is homeless in His Own universe except as we make room for Him in our hearts.

So on this Thanksgiving weekend, let us write a bread-and-butter note to God:

Dear Father:

What language shall I borrow, to thank Thee for all Thy favors? I have spent the whole long weekend of my life in Your house. The appointments are vast and wonderful, from green earth to blue sky, from atom to universe. And to think that You would make it all available to me!

I must tell You how sorry I am for ways I have misused Your hospitality. I have treated some hours as if life were cheap, by spending them thoughtlessly and thanklessly; I've treated still others as if life were contemptible, by hating and complaining. I've not always been true to my body or my mind, nor to friendship

116

or beauty or opportunity.

Please forgive me, Gracious Host.

I know that I can never deserve such hospitality as You have shown. But this I would do: I would return the invitation. You have entertained me in the mansion of Your creation; now I invite You into the poor hovel of my heart. Come in, Father, and make my heart Your home.

Sincerely and gratefully,
ELLSWORTH.

And now, what bread and butter note would you like to write to God?

117

At hope's end, a love-light . . .

Even the best of human love has its limits, because we human beings are limited. Our love is likely to fall short because it is usually tinged with self-interest, or because we haven't the power to help in the measure in which we are needed. And ultimately our best human love has to fall short simply because we die; thus it is that people sometimes feel, in the grief of bereavement, that they have been betrayed by their friend or spouse's passing.

Is there, then, any love in this universe that will never fall short? Is there a love that can leap the boundaries of time, space, and changing fortune? Yes, the Gospel and the Creed answer; indeed, there is!

How Far Does God's Love Reach?

There is a phrase in the Apostles' Creed which speaks to me more powerfully than any other. It's possible, however, that even if you have repeated this Creed hundreds of times, you may never have heard this phrase; for if you have recited the Creed only in a United Methodist service, you would not know that this powerful phrase belongs to the Creed. It is the most bewildering portion of the Creed, I'm sure, and the one least often preached about; yet it seems to me to tell us, better than any other, the magnificent quality of the heart and character of God.

I am speaking of the four words, *He descended into hell.* They come in the portion of the Creed which celebrates the ministry of our Lord Jesus Christ, in this fashion: ". . . suffered under Pontius Pilate, was crucified, dead, and buried; He descended into hell; the third day He rose from the dead . . ."

These words were omitted from our American Methodist use of the Creed with some reason, since they apparently came into the Creed quite late. That is, these words are not to be found in the earliest manuscripts of the Apostles' Creed. In fact, the first extant manuscript in which they appear comes to us from the year 570 A.D., according to our best research. It ought to be said, however, that the phrase appeared in other Christian creeds, and that it has a basis in the Scriptures themselves.

As a United Methodist minister, I often wanted to preach about these four words, but hesitated to do so since they were not in the Creed as we commonly use it. Then, on my first visit to London, England, my soul was set free. I went, as almost any Methodist minister visiting England would, to Wesley's Chapel on City Road, the church where John Wesley spent the last years of his life. At the front of the church the Apostles' Creed was painted, in letters large enough for the worshipping congregation to read. To my surprise and delight, I saw that it included the phrase which I had loved for so long: "He descended into hell." If it's good enough for the 'Mother Church' of Methodism, I said to myself, it ought to have something in it for *all* Methodists; therefore, I would rejoice in it from the pulpit just as I had for some years in the privacy of my soul.

This phrase means so much to me because it tells us so powerfully what God is like. When the creed begins, in its staccato, sledgehammer fashion, to declare its faith in Jesus Christ, it makes very clear that the Church knows that this Jesus is very God of very God.

> "I believe in God the Father Almighty, maker of heaven and earth; and in Jesus Christ His only Son our Lord; who was conceived by the Holy Spirit, born of the Virgin Mary . . . ."

Now—what will such an One as this do: One whose name is mentioned in the same breath with God, described as His only Son, and declared to have come to earth by extraordinary conception and birth: what will such an One as this do? The next words tell us, with excruciating power:

"suffered under Pontius Pilate, was crucified, dead, and buried;" Hard words, these, for a God: "suffered . . . crucified . . . dead . . . buried . . ." These, after all, are words for the human creature. They are the cramping, frustrating, ball-and-chain words of humanity. They are the very words from which we would like to escape, the words which constantly remind us that we are human beings, and not God.

Yet these are the words and experiences that God's Son takes to Himself: suffered, crucified, dead, buried. As we repeat these words, we begin to feel the measure of God's love, that His Son would lay aside the privileges and prerogatives of heaven and take upon Himself all the normal anguish of humankind. Yes, and *more* than is normal or average.

Nevertheless, something in us says, "This isn't really far enough. True, the mark of humanity includes suffering, death, and burial; these are the issues which fence us in. But we face still a worse prospect. What about hell?"

And so the great Creed goes the limit:

". . . He descended into hell . . ."

This is the kind of God He is. He follows us all the way. He pursues us to the limit.

The idea is so strange, so beyond our conceiving, that we want first of all to know if it has any basis in the Scriptures. As a matter of fact, it does, in a rather wide variety of places. Most of the references are shrouded in mystical, poetic language, but in total they begin to reach us. Peter touches the matter in the first Christian sermon, on the Day of Pentecost, when he explains to the multitude that the words of the Psalmist David refer prophetically to Jesus, when he wrote, "Thou wilt not leave my soul in hell, neither wilt thou suffer thine Holy One to see

123

corruption."[1] The Apostle Paul makes an oblique reference in Romans 10, but it sheds little additional light for us. More significant, perhaps, is a reference in the Epistle to the Ephesians, where the apostle explains that before Christ's ascension, he "descended first into the lower parts of the earth," and that in this process "he led captivity captive."[2]

The First Epistle of Peter uses a more revealing figure of speech, when it speaks of Christ having "preached unto the spirits in prison,"[3] and again when he notes, "For this cause was the gospel preached also to them that are dead, that they might be judged according to men in the flesh, but live according to God in the spirit."[4] This passage pretty clearly is telling us that during the three days Jesus was in the grave, he went to the abode of the dead, to Hades, to offer the inhabitants a way of salvation.

What is the meaning of this strange picture? I find two things here. First, there is insight for a perplexing theological problem; and then, a message of hope for the day-to-day life each of us leads.

Most of us, unfortunately, miss the grandeur of these somewhat enigmatic passages of Scripture and the Creedal phrase which springs from them. So often we are too literalistic. We stumble over the great truth which lies before us because we're uneasy about the vessel in which the truth is delivered. Dr. William Barclay rightly reminds us that this part of the Creed is "the language of hope and of devotion and of vision and of poetry."[5] If we will remember that, we will find insight which will inspire and uplift us.

First, the theological problem. Jesus said, during His earthly ministry, "I am the door . . . I am the Way." In one of the first

124

Christian sermons Peter declared, "And there is salvation in no one else, for there is no other name under heaven given among men by which we must be saved."[6] The early Church believed that there was no salvation except in Jesus Christ. He was The Way. But inevitably a question arose: if salvation was possible only through Him, what about those generations that had lived before the Cross? how could they be saved?

And four New Testament letters—Romans, Ephesians, and First and Second Peter—offered an answer. They concluded from certain Old Testament prophecies that their Lord had gone to Hades, the abode of the dead, during the three days between His death and resurrection, to preach to the departed souls there. Peter's letter calls them "the spirits in prison." When Paul reports on the same occasion in his letter to the Ephesians, he pictures a scene of triumph: Christ ascending to heaven with a host of "captives" He had won in His preaching to the dead.

Now you can respond to this New Testament theology by saying that it is primitive—for it is. But remember that 'primitive' is not necessarily a bad word; it may mean closer to the source, and therefore nearer the truth. You can say that it was meant to be interpreted symbolically—and perhaps it was. But let us not become so enamoured of the modern mind that we rob ourselves of the benefit of ancient wisdom and eternal truth. The New Testament and the Apostles' Creed are telling us that there are no limitations upon the grace of God or the Lordship of Christ.

"What about the thousands who lived and died before Calvary?" we ask. And it is as if the Creed replies, "The grace of God can

125

reach even these; for even the dead are encompassed by the Lordship of Christ. Because He suffered death, He could go to the place of the dead. As surely as He became the Savior of the living by walking and eating and working among the living, just so certainly He became the Savior of the dead by accepting the limitations of the dead. No corner of this universe is outside His reach, because He will not let it be. No pit of hell is too deep, no level of Hades too dim and shaded. The Lord who suffered, was crucified, dead, and buried, also 'descended into hell.' There are no limitations upon His pursuit of humanity. Not even death can take us beyond the grace of God and the Lordship of Jesus Christ. His kingdom extends from the underworld of Hades to the eternity of God's throne."

I think I would be stretching a point if I were to assume that the same idea would apply to the dead since Calvary. But from what the Creed and the Scriptures say about those whose opportunity was limited before Calvary, perhaps we have a basis for trying to understand God's attitude toward the human race since Calvary. We are often asked, "What about those who have never heard the Gospel? Will they be shut out of the Kingdom, when they haven't even had a chance to decide?" Obviously, I cannot give a final answer to that question; such judgments, ultimately, are the province of God alone. But this much can be said: If God's sense of fairness provided an opportunity to those who had died before Calvary, as the Scriptures seem to indicate, will He not also provide fair data of choice for every human being? Will not the judge of all the earth do right? I do not know how God will make such provision, but I think I may rightly conclude that He will give opportunity for all. He pursues us to the uttermost. Each human creature must have his or her chance.

That's the theological insight. When I recite the words, "He descended into hell," I remind myself of the profound hunger of God for our human souls. He allows no boundary to shut out His love. Each soul will have fair and ultimate opportunity, even if God must go to hell to provide it.

And then there is the present, day-by-day world in which you and I live. This phrase from the Creed tells me that there is no human experience which is beyond the compassion of our Lord, no terror of human suffering He has not known, no agony with which He cannot sympathize. In the dense blackness of sickness, bereavement, temptation or defeat, we cry out, "This is *hell*!"—and the Creed answers, "He descended into hell." He knows what you and I feel. He has been there before us. Nothing that we experience is beyond His comprehension.

It has been more than thirty years, but I shall never forget a man with whom I worked on the night shift of a factory office at the Allis Chalmers Company in Milwaukee. I was working my way through college, but my friend Earl was simply making a living. Life had dealt him a mean hand. He had the heart and soul of a teacher, perhaps even of a true scholar, but he didn't have the education to qualify him for a teaching job. He took other work, but of course he was a misfit in other jobs. During the depression of the 1930's, when even the well-qualified found themselves out of work, Earl was soon unemployed, and at last found himself a ward of the County relief program.

He told me one evening, half-bitterly, half-pathetically, of the winter day he was carrying surplus food home in a coaster wagon. It was humiliating to trudge down the street, pulling a child's wagon of cans with their tell-tale white labels. But to climax his shame, he slipped on the ice and fell, overturning the coaster wagon and canned goods, just as some friends drove by—friends who still had an automobile—and called out, "It's hell, Earl, isn't it?" And Earl, bitter in his shame and in the knowledge that his friends really had no idea how miserable it was, called back, "You're damn right it's hell!"

So it is, sometimes, in your experience and mine. In the poverty of our failure, we stumble and sprawl on the pavement of life; and as we sit in the disarray of our dreams, with our childish hopes and our confused despair spread around us in absurd confusion, we lift our heads and cry, "This is hell!" And a voice from heaven whispers back, *"He descended into hell."*

Hear me: walk into any of the hell of life, and you will find that He is there before you. In a room where a woman waits for cancer to make its last monstrous claim, in a cheap hotel room where an alcoholic agonizes for just one drink, in a luxury apartment where a man and a woman sit in the misery of a crumbling marriage . . . someone cries out, "God what a hell this is!"—and heaven says, so quietly, *"He* descended into hell."

This is why I cherish the words we American Methodists have dropped from the ancient Creed. No part of the Creed tells me a more important fact about God than does this: the day-to-day fact that when we human beings pass through our private hell, we are sustained by One who "descended into hell . . ." and the theological fact that the reach of God's grace and the lordship of Jesus Christ is beyond our fathoming. Not even death or Hades are out of His province, for He has chosen to invade even their domains in His hunger for the souls of our race.

Ask me, then, what God is like, this God whom I worship—and I will answer with the sledgehammer brevity of the Creed:

"He descended into hell."

So, I worship Him. So, I love Him.

References

Chapter one: *Honey in the Lion*
1. Judges 14:14
2. 2 Corinthians 12:9

Chapter two: *The Three Great Books*
1. Jessamyn West, *To See the Dream*, p. 3
2. Elton Trueblood, *The Company of the Committed*, p. 41
3. Psalm 90:2b, 4a, 12 (RSV)

Chapter four: *Can God Be Good When Life Is Bad?*
1. Romans 8:28 (RSV)
2. Romans 5:3,4 (RSV)

Chapter five: *To Whom It May Concern*
1. Genesis 16:13
2. Judges 6:24
3. Acts 17:22, 23 (RSV)
4. Acts 17:27b, 28 (RSV)

Chapter six: *The Tongue and I*
1. Proverbs 18:21 (KJV)
2. Proverbs 10:19 (KJV)
3. Proverbs 10:19 (The Living Bible)
4. Matthew 12:37
5. Isaiah 6:5 (RSV)

Chapter seven: *I've Gotta Be Me?*
1. "I've Gotta Be Me," by Walter Marks. Damila Music, Inc., 1967
2. Romans 7:15, 24
3. 1 John 3:2
4. Trevor H. Davies, "The Everlasting Mercy," *The Christian Advocate*, 7-15-20, p. 956

Chapter nine: *Books That Babies Can Read*
1. O. Spurgeon English and Gerald Pearson, *Emotional Problems of Living*, p. 23
2. Exodus 20:5 (RSV)

Chapter ten: *When the Trees Held an Election*
1. Judges 8:28 (RSV)
2. Judges 9:8-15 (RSV)
3. *Interpreters Dictionary of the Bible*, Vol. III, p. 596
4. *Interpreters Bible,* Vol. II, p. 754
5. Barbara Tuchman, *Esquire*, May, 1980, p. 27 (Adapted from a lecture delivered at the U.S. Military Academy)
6. *Time*, 7-26-68

Chapter eleven: *A Bread and Butter Note to God*
1. Katharine Butler Hathaway, *The Little Locksmith*, p. 229
2. Emily Post, *Etiquette*, p. 468
3. Hathaway, *op.cit.*, pp. 234, 235
4. Psalm 4:1b (RSV)
5. Psalm 31:8 (KJV)

Chapter twelve: *How Far Does God's Love Reach?*
1. Acts 2:27
2. Ephesians 4:8-10
3. 1 Peter 3:18-20
4. 1 Peter 4:6
5. William Barclay, *The Apostles Creed for Everyman*, p. 133
6. Acts 4:12 (RSV)

132